Sew Darn Cute

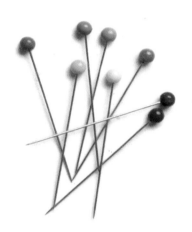

Jenny Ryan

Photography by
Bill Milne

ST. MARTIN'S GRIFFIN
NEW YORK

Sew Darn Cute

30 Sweet & Simple Projects to Sew & Embellish

A Quirk Packaging Book
Design by woolypear
Developmental editing by Sarah Scheffel
Technical editing by Erin Slonaker
Illustrations by Johnny Ryan

Library of Congress Cataloging-in-Publication Data Available Upon Request

ISBN-13: 978-0-312-38383-1
ISBN-10: 0-312-38383-5

First Edition: February 2009

10 9 8 7 6 5 4 3 2 1

For Johnny

My role model, partner in crime, and best friend.

Contents

ssssS...

Introduction

Welcome to *Sew Darn Cute!* Within these pages you'll find step-by-step instructions for thirty unique projects ranging from housewares to baby goods and crafty organizers to ladylike accessories. You'll learn to customize your creations using some of my favorite embellishing methods, such as simple embroidery and appliqué. And I'll share tips and techniques for combining new and vintage fabrics to sew one-of-a-kind items to keep or give. The tricks I've picked up over a lifetime of crafting are now yours, and I can't wait to see what you'll do with them.

Home Ec classes had been all but phased out by the time I got to high school, so everything I learned about sewing and embellishing was picked up on the fly. A childhood summer spent at my Aunt Jean's house taught me to make a quilted patchwork pillow, while hanging out with high school friends often involved painting the names of punk bands onto leather jackets or chopping a few inches from the hem of a secondhand dress to make it more flattering. The urge to make things by hand never left me, and eventually I found myself sewing so much I opened a website so I could sell my creations to the world at large. Surrounded by friends who were doing the same, I was then inspired to start a craft fair here in Los Angeles called Felt Club. While I sometimes wonder if I'd be a better seamstress if I'd learned things in a more formal, structured way, I think the way I did go about it—by absorbing ideas and tips from various friends and family members over the years—has helped make me more open-minded and experimental.

My main point is this: There's no right or wrong way to approach sewing. The hardest part is just getting started, and everything else is the rickrack on top. Yes, practice does make perfect, but who says "perfect" is even what you should be going for? Sewing is a fantastic way to mellow out, to spend time with friends, and to express your individuality. Remember that you're supposed to be having fun! Every step of the process is a chance to show your creativity, from choosing your favorite fabrics and devising or altering sewing patterns to selecting the trims and buttons that make a project feel like it's really yours.

Not to mention: Sewing is incredibly empowering! You're no longer at the whim of manufacturers or trends when you learn how to make things yourself. Making time to be creative truly is the gift that keeps on giving. Nothing beats the fun of holding regular craft nights with your pals or bestowing a thoughtful handmade gift on someone you love. You could even start up your own blog and post a tutorial for the latest project you've dreamed up. These are all ways of fostering self-expression and a feeling of community, which to me is what being a crafter is all about.

This book is intended for sewers at all skill levels. Some projects are quite simple, while others may get a bit tricky, but if you follow the instructions, step-by-step, you can make your way through them all. Start with an easy project like the 4-in-1 Headband (page 38) and you'll be sporting one in no time flat—or set aside a long afternoon to work on the Spumoni Stripe Quilt (page 106), and you'll have an heirloom-quality gift for the next baby shower you attend. I share plenty of tips along the way, and there's no end to the variations you can create by mixing and matching fabrics and embellishments. My hope is that you'll try new techniques, flex your artistic muscles, and push yourself beyond what you might think you're capable of. Once you do, you'll start to see a world full of possibilities and will wonder: What can I stitch up next?

Jenny Ryan

www.sewdarncute.com

Tools & Techniques

Here is an overview of all the basic tools and notions I like to keep at the ready in my sewing room. You don't need to run out and purchase every single item; you can acquire them gradually as you come across a need for them. For a shortlist of tools you must have to complete the projects in this book, see Basic Sewing Tools, page 15.

BASIC SEWING TOOLS & NOTIONS

Dressmaker's Shears A good pair of 8" bent-handled dressmaker's shears are a tool you'll use constantly, so buy the best quality pair you can find—Gingher is an excellent choice. I like to write "FABRIC ONLY" on the blades of my shears with a permanent marker so they won't ever be used to cut paper or anything else that might dull the blades.

Embroidery Scissors These small, fine-tipped scissors are wonderful for snipping away threads when doing detailed embroidery work. As a bonus, they're usually cute, too! I like to loop a long ribbon through mine, to wear around my neck as I work. My favorite pink-handled pair comes from SublimeStitching.com.

Small Sewing Scissors Keep a pair of sewing scissors on hand for clipping stray threads, cutting into tight corners on fabric appliqué pieces, or cutting notches into fabric curves. These should also be used only on fabric and thread, never on paper or plastic. I highly recommend the Fiskars Micro-Tip 5" Scissors, which have extra-fine angled blade tips—they're the best I've found yet.

Plain/Regular Scissors Keep a pair of run-of-the-mill scissors on hand for cutting out paper patterns or anything else you need to snip that isn't fabric. Keep these close at hand so you're never tempted to use your "good" scissors for something you shouldn't!

Pinking Shears These specialty shears cut with a zigzag edge, which can help prevent fraying when used on woven fabrics. They can also lend a decorative look when used to cut non-fraying fabrics like felt.

Dressmaker's Shears

28mm Rotary Cutter

Embroidery Scissors

Small Sewing Scissors

Rotary Cutter The rotary cutter is hands-down my favorite tool to use when I have a lot of sewing to do—it's especially handy to use when making a quilt. (If you only buy one, get the versatile 45mm size—though a smaller, 28mm version can be handy for cutting small appliqué pieces.) These rolling cutters have extremely sharp, retractable blades and are able to slice through several layers of fabric at once. It may help to practice on some scrap fabric at first, until you get a feel for using it. I use my rotary cutter in conjunction with a clear quilting ruler. Remember to always, always keep the safety guard on when the rotary cutter is not in use. You can also purchase rotary cutters with blades that cut zigzags or scallops, which are fun to use for felt-based projects.

Self-Healing Cutting Mat I have two of these, which I use to cover my dining room table when I'm doing a big bout of sewing. They have a non-slip surface that is perfect for laying out fabrics and will protect your table when using the rotary cutter. The measurements printed along the mat can also be extremely useful when you're sizing up pattern pieces. I'd recommend buying the largest size you can afford—at least 18" x 24". They're large but flat, so they're easy to stash behind a bookcase or flat on a high shelf when not in use.

Seam Ripper We all make mistakes, so we all need a seam ripper. These pointy wonders are great for picking out unwanted stitches, and the curved blade part can also be used to slice buttonholes open.

Template Plastic These are transparent sheets of plastic available in varying thicknesses, which work great for tracing out pattern pieces, appliqué shapes, and the like. Since the plastic is clear, you can place it over any shape, trace, and cut. They are easily cut with regular scissors or an X-Acto knife.

Plastic Ruler For most measuring and cutting jobs, I reach for a clear plastic quilting ruler. You'll find a ruler that is at least 18" long and 2–3" wide to be the most useful.

Tape Measure When you need to measure something that isn't flat, a tape measure will do the trick handily. Most are made of flexible plastic and are easy to roll up and stash in your pocket—maybe the pocket of your Pockets Aplenty Apron (page 118)?

Magnetic Seam Guide When you first begin sewing, you may find yourself worrying about whether or not you're leaving the proper seam allowance. A magnetic seam guide is a tool that sticks to the metal throat plate of your sewing machine, providing a straight edge for you to butt the fabric against while you sew.

Tailor's Chalk These are handheld pieces of clay-based chalk that are used to trace patterns onto fabric; they come in a variety of colors. I usually use blue for light fabrics and white for dark fabrics. The chalk is easily brushed off afterward, or you can also give it a swipe or dab with a damp washcloth. You can also buy refillable chalk markers, called Chaco Liners, that are easier to hold than a blunt square of chalk and make a more precise line.

Thread

Disappearing-Ink Marker There are two kinds of disappearing-ink marking pens: air-soluble and water-soluble. The latter can be removed using a damp cloth, while the former disappears over time. The packages will usually tell you that air-soluble pen marks will evaporate within 48–72 hours, but in my experience it usually happens much faster. This can vary wildly though, depending on factors like air quality and the type of fabric you're using—so always test on a piece of scrap fabric first.

Press Cloth This is simply a piece of cotton fabric you'll use to protect your work when pressing, which comes in very handy when ironing on appliqués and the like. You can buy these pre-made, but I usually use a plain white flour sack dishtowel.

Ironing Board and Pad You know that flimsy ironing board pad that came with your sewing machine? It's not gonna cut it. Invest in a thicker cover and pull it right over the first one. Trust me when I say you'll end up with ugly marks all over your pretty fabric if you use the thinner pad, which simply doesn't provide enough protection between the metal frame of the ironing board and the iron. What you're looking for here is thickness.

Steam Iron You don't have to buy a top-of-the-line iron that costs as much as a small car, but you don't want something that's going to fizzle out, either. Choose a nice, mid-range model that allows you to turn the steam action on and off, since sometimes you need a dry iron to fuse adhesives.

Sleeve Board or Point Presser A sleeve board is basically a long, narrow mini ironing board that works very well for pressing seams open and for pressing curves. I also love using a point presser, a lesser-known tool made of wood that I first discovered when a friend gave me one her Grandpa made. Used by tailors, these tools are wonderful for pressing seams flat, steaming fabric without scorching (as the wood holds steam from the iron), and to create perfectly pressed corners and points. They can be hard to find, but I've seen them online at www.sews.com.

Hand-Sewing Needles Any sewing shop will have a variety pack of hand-sewing needles (sometimes called *sharps*) available, and any one of these packs will work fine for most purposes. The only exception is if you're going to be embroidering something, in which case you'll want to buy a pack of sharp-pointed embroidery needles.

Straight Pins

Sewing Machine Needles Always use the appropriate needles for your particular sewing machine and the project you're working on. Most of the projects in this book can be made with a standard size 12 needle—but if you're working with heavyweight or multi-layered fabrics, you'll want to move up to a size 16 or so. When in doubt, read the fine print and ask a salesperson.

Straight Pins Pick up a box of standard dressmaker pins and you'll be all set. I prefer pins with colorful glass balls on the end. They're quick to grab hold of when you need to remove them, easy to spot if you drop them, and they won't melt if you move an iron too close (unlike plastic-head pins).

Pincushion You'll want to keep at least two pincushions on hand. I like a decorative (but still useful!) pincushion to keep on the shelf with the rest of my sewing notions, plus a magnetic pincushion to keep right next to my sewing machine. The latter makes it very easy to keep track of stray pins as I remove them, and I can also wave it over the floor to pick up any I've dropped. If I'm doing some hand-sewing in front of the TV, I'll wear the Wrist Pincushion on page 126.

Thread Polyester or cotton-wrapped polyester thread is the best to use for most sewing—my favorite brand is Gutermann, but Coats & Clark All-Purpose thread works well too. Choose a thread marked "Sew-All" or "All Purpose" (rather than a hand-quilting thread) or risk having it fray or bunch up in the machine.

Turning Tools Many crafters use what's called a loop turner, which is a long piece of wire with a hook at one end, for turning fabric tubes (such as straps-to-be) right side out. Simply insert the wire into the fabric tube, hook the end over your fabric, and pull the hooked end back through so the tube is right side out. These are commonly available at sewing stores—as is my personal favorite, Dritz "Quick Turn" fabric tube turners. The Quick Turn tool is a two-part device consisting of a hollow plastic tube you insert into your fabric tube, and a wooden dowel you then push through the plastic.

Snaps Snaps have "male" and "female" halves, and you can find ones that you stitch on by hand or ones that are attached more securely with an inexpensive snap-setting tool, which consists of a metal rod and plastic anvil that are used in conjunction with a hammer to affix the snaps to fabric. My absolute favorite kind of snap-setting tool is made by SnapSource and is called The SnapSetter™. This three-part tool holds the snaps in place while you hammer them in—meaning it's easy to use as well as foolproof.

Wrist Pincushion

EMBELLISHING TOOLS & NOTIONS

HeatnBond Fusible Adhesive This fusible adhesive is sold in sheets or on a roll—the adhesive melts with the heat of your iron and is used to bond fabrics together. One side is shiny, the other side is paper. You'll iron the adhesive to the wrong side of a piece of fabric, then trace your appliqué template on the paper side. Cut out the appliqué, peel off the paper backing, and stick the appliqué adhesive-side down onto the item you're embellishing. Iron to fuse, following the manufacturer's instructions. HeatnBond comes in "Lite" and "Ultra" strengths.

Bias Tape Maker You can buy pre-made bias tape at any craft store, but bias tape you've made yourself can really give your projects that extra bit of oomph—and making it yourself means you can use any kind of beautiful printed fabric. See page 18 for instructions. Also, store-bought bias tape is usually made from a 50/50 poly-cotton blend, which can look cheap and stiff.

Bias Tape Maker

Bias tape makers are available at most sewing shops (usually in the quilting section) and in several different sizes—the one I use most often makes 1" wide bias tape, which I then fold in half and press to create double-fold bias tape. This is the exact type used throughout this book, to trim projects like the Happy Hostess Dishtowels (page 82) and the Dainty Doll Quilt (page 104). Bias tape makers basically look like flattened metal cone-shaped tubes. Feed a strip of fabric into the wide end of the tube, then pull it out at the small end and press flat with an iron as you go. It's easy!

If the project you're working on has a lot of rounded edges, you will want to cut your fabric strips the traditional way, on the bias (at a 45-degree angle). This gives the tape enough stretch to lie smoothly over curved areas. It is sometimes helpful to pre-press the bias tape around the curves before you stitch it down. However, you can also use a bias tape maker to create straight (non-stretchy) binding, which works nicely for projects with a lot of right angles. Just use the bias tape maker as you normally would, cutting the fabric on the grain instead of at an angle.

Yo-Yo Maker You can create fabric yo-yos without a yo-yo maker—people have been doing it for years—but I love that Clover is now making these handy plastic doo-dads. Using a yo-yo maker ensures that your yo-yo will be perfectly circular, and the stitching guides help you achieve the ideal stitch length, meaning the fabric will bunch up just right. These are available in many sizes (the one I use most often makes a 2⅜" yo-yo) and even shapes like flowers and hearts.

Free-Motion Quilting Hoop Pick up a few embroidery hoops (small and medium sizes are best) to use for free-motion quilting. It will keep the fabric secure as you sew and is easy to grip as you move the fabric around under the needle. I'd recommend a plastic hoop for sturdiness, as the cheaper unfinished wooden hoops can sometimes break.

Yo-Yo

Yo-Yo Makers

Iron-On Vinyl Iron-on vinyl allows you to "laminate" fabric, giving it a water-resistant vinyl finish. It is available in glossy or matte finishes and can be sewn through after ironing. It can be used on fabric or paper and is usually sold in 1- or 2-yard rolls.

Embroidery Floss Six-stranded cotton thread used for embroidering details onto your work—DMC is the most common brand and, in my experience, is the easiest to use. It's cheap, too—often you can pick up four skeins for a dollar. If you'd like to stitch finer lines, just separate the strands and use three or four instead of six. Another thread you might try using is pearl cotton, which has a slightly shiny finish but isn't divisible like normal embroidery floss.

Covered Button Kits These kits include metal button blanks with a rubber mold and pushing tool. Each kit comes with a circle template on the back of the package, which you use to cut out the fabric of your choice. Following the directions on the package, you'll use the pushing tool and rubber mold to wrap the fabric around the metal button blank and attach the back shank piece. These kits are extremely easy to use and come in a wide variety of sizes. If the fabric you want to use is sheer or thin, iron some light interfacing to the wrong side of the fabric first—otherwise the shiny metal surface of the button blank will show through.

BASIC SEWING TOOLS

Here's a quick-reference list of the essential tools you'll need as you make the projects in this book.

Cutting Tools

☐ Dressmaker's shears

☐ Embroidery scissors

☐ Small sewing scissors

☐ Regular scissors

☐ Rotary cutter

☐ Self-healing mat

☐ Plastic ruler

Measuring and Marking Tools

☐ Tape measure

☐ Tailor's chalk

☐ Marking pen

☐ Pins

Finishing Tools

☐ Iron

☐ Ironing board

☐ Press cloth

☐ Turning tool

SEWING MACHINE ACCESSORIES

Non-Stick Foot (also called Teflon Foot) Sewing fabrics like vinyl or oilcloth can be difficult, since they're apt to bunch up under the sewing machine's normal metal feet. A non-stick foot will move smoothly over problematic fabrics like these, allowing you to keep your stitches even and consistent.

Darning Foot This sewing machine attachment is a necessity for free-motion quilting. It encircles the needle without putting any pressure on the fabric below, which allows you to move the fabric around freely, guiding it in any direction.

SEWING & EMBELLISHING BASICS

Making a Yo-Yo Use a yo-yo maker (see page 14) or make a circle-shaped template, which you can draw on template plastic or a piece of stiff paper (like cardstock). The circle you draw should be drawn twice as big as you'd like the yo-yo to be, plus about ¼". Here's what to do after you've drawn and cut your template:

With a disappearing-ink marker or pencil, trace the circle onto the wrong side of the fabric, then cut.

Holding the circle with the wrong side facing you, begin folding the edges over toward the wrong side by ¼". Sew along the edge using a running stitch, keeping your stitches close to the fold. (Be sure to use at least 10–12" of thread so you don't run out halfway around the circle.)

Once you reach the starting point, pull on the thread until the edges pucker up tightly and meet in the center. Make a few stitches to secure, then knot and cut your thread.

Squash the yo-yo flat so the hole is in the center, and you're done! Your yo-yo can be used as is—or sew a button or large bead to the center to add a little something extra.

Free-Motion Quilting Sometimes sewing straight lines gets boring, and you may want to decorate your projects with some curly loop-de-loop patterns instead. For this, you can turn to free-motion quilting. You'll have to pick up a darning (or free-motion) foot, and use that instead of the normal presser foot. Once you've attached the darning foot, switch your stitch length to 0 and lower your feed dogs (your manual will tell you how). In most sewing, the feed dogs (those two ribbed bars under the presser foot) are what move your fabric forward or backward through the machine. With free-motion quilting, however, you lower the feed dogs so the only thing moving the fabric around under the needle is you.

TIPS

✱ Free-motion work isn't just for stitching together quilt layers. You can cover any fabric you like with crazy stitching, just keep in mind that it should be somewhat stiff so you can move it around easily. Pick up some tear-away stabilizer (found in the notions department) and apply that to the wrong side of your fabric to temporarily stiffen it while you're sewing.

✱ I used to be intimidated by free-motion quilting until I saw it done right in front of me at a sewing machine shop. If you're the same way there are some great how-to videos for beginners on YouTube. Seeing something demonstrated first can be the push you need to give it a try.

Free-Motion Quilting

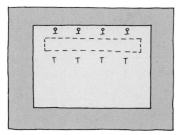

step 2

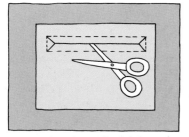

step 3

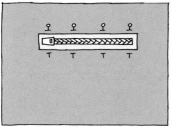

step 5.1

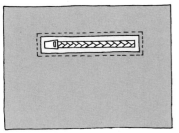

step 5.2

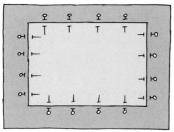

step 6

Create a "quilt sandwich" to practice on, made from two squares of scrap fabric with some batting in the middle (12" x 12" is a good size). You can secure the layers together inside an embroidery hoop, or just join with safety pins at the edges. An embroidery hoop gives you something to hold as you move the fabric around under the needle, or you can purchase rubberized quilter's gloves to help you keep your grip.

To get started, just insert the fabric sandwich under the needle. Lower the darning foot. Hold the thread and use the hand wheel to lower the needle and take a couple of slow stitches to get started. Then, let go of the thread and just start sewing. Think of the needle as a pen you can sketch with—try writing your name, drawing spirals, making loops—whatever you like. If you want to create detailed designs, just keep practicing. As a nice bonus, you can cut up your practice squares later on and trim them with bias tape to create fun potholders.

Inserting a Zippered Pocket Take your bags and totes to the next level by inserting a zippered pocket into the interior. I promise it's easier than you think! Try putting a pocket inside your Pillowcase Purse (page 54) or Sweet Treat Tote (page 50)—just remember you'll be inserting the pocket to one of the lining pieces *before* you sew the two lining pieces together. You'll need:

One 7" zipper

Two pieces of 9½" x 6½" cotton fabric

Two pieces of 9½" x 6½" fusible interfacing

1 Fuse the interfacing to the wrong side(s) of your pocket pieces.

2 Place one pocket piece right side down onto one piece of your bag's lining. Measure the length of your zipper's teeth and draw a rectangle onto the pocket piece that is the length of the zipper and ½" high. Draw this box 1½" down from the top of the pocket piece.

3 Pin the pocket piece into place and sew around all edges of the rectangle. Then use a ruler to mark a line down the center of the rectangle you sewed, and cut through both layers of fabric, angling into the corners at the ends.

4 Pull the pocket piece through to the back of the lining piece and press flat.

5 Pin the zipper into place, then sew around all edges of the rectangular opening you made, stitching about ⅛" from the edge. Take your time sewing and remove pins as needed while you go. If you find the pins too bulky, you can tape the zipper down with Scotch tape—that's how I prefer to do it.

6 Place the bag's lining right side down and pin the second pocket piece to the first, with right sides together. Sew around all edges of the pocket.

Bias Tape 101 Attaching bias tape may seem tricky, but don't let that stop you from experimenting—practice really does make perfect. Here are my favorite ways to use it:

On projects with straight edges, such as the Happy Hostess Dishtowels (page 82), you'll start attaching trim in the middle of one side. Let's use the dishtowels as an example, keeping in mind you can use these instructions for any straight-edged item you're sewing.

1   With the towel facing right side up, lay the bias tape right side down and fold open so one raw edge of the tape is aligned with the edge of the towel. Pin into place all the way to the first corner.

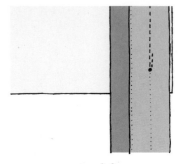

steps 1–3

2   Begin sewing about ½" from the starting point of the tape, stitching in the first fold line down from the edge. After sewing about an inch or so, fold the un-sewn ½" toward the needle, and backstitch to secure.

3   Continue sewing down the bias tape, stopping when you get ¼" from the first corner, and backstitch.

4   Take the towel out of the machine and fold the remaining bias tape up, creating a 90-degree angle from the towel's corner and the left edge of the bias tape.

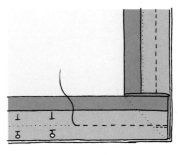

step 6

5   Fold the tape back down over the fold you just made. Your fold should be even with the top of the towel, and the right-hand side of the bias tape should be aligned with the edge of the towel.

6   Pin into place and continue sewing along that first fold line closest to the towel's edge, starting at the folded corner edge you made in step 5.

7   Continue this process around all edges of the towel. When you reach the starting point, pause for a moment to cut the end of the bias tape so that it overlaps your starting point by ½". Pin down and sew edges closed.

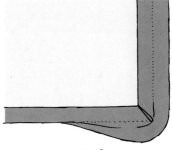

step 8

8   Next, start folding the bias tape over toward the wrong side of your towel, pinning and hand-stitching it into place with a blind stitch. You'll see that as you fold the tape over, the corners will form nice angles—they are referred to as "mitered" corners. If you need help mitering the back corners, just fold and press them into place.

9   If you'd rather not do all that hand-stitching on the back (and who could blame you?), skip the hand-stitching and machine-sew the tape into place after folding it over and pinning. Use a coordinating thread, and sew it with the back side facing you so you're sure you catch all the layers. Sewing it about ⅛" from the inside edge of the tape will usually do the trick.

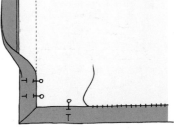

step 9

On projects with rounded edges, such as the Custom Vinyl Bib (page 101), I just slip the raw edge of the item inside the bias tape and sew through all the layers, stitching about ⅛" from the inside edge of the tape. I don't usually pin these projects into place, as I find it easier to manipulate and stretch the tape around rounded edges without pins getting in the way. Just sew it on slowly, and be sure to use bias tape that has been made the traditional way, with fabric strips cut at a 45-degree angle.

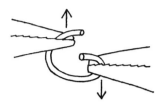

Attaching Charms

Attaching Charms It's fun to perk up a plain zipper with a dangly charm or two, as shown on the Terrycloth Travel Pouch (page 62). All you need is your charm, plus a jump ring and two pairs of small jewelry (or other small) pliers.

1 With a pair of pliers in each hand, hold the jump ring with the split part facing up and centered.

2 Move one hand toward you and one away from you at the same time.

3 Slip the charm onto the open ring, then slip the ring through the zipper pull opening.

4 Repeat step 2 in reverse to close.

Running Stitch

BASIC HAND STITCHES

Running Stitch Evenly sized and spaced stitches—very basic.

Hidden Stitch I use a tiny overhand stitch to join edges together. Using coordinating thread means it will barely be visible. Insert needle diagonally from back edge to front, picking up just a bit of fabric each time.

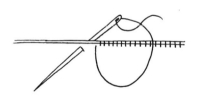

Hidden Stitch

Whipstitch Similar to the hidden stitch, but larger and more visible—and you'll insert the needle at a right angle.

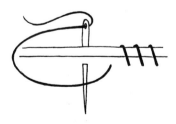

Whipstitch

Charm

Buttons

TRICKS OF THE TRADE

Keep a Clean Machine It seems like a no-brainer—that cleaning and oiling your machine on a regular basis will keep it running smoothly—and yet it's something many crafters neglect to do. Give it a quick once-over every time you complete a sewing project, and you and your machine will both be a lot happier!

1   Gather up the following supplies and keep them in a fun vintage basket or lunchbox in your work area:

> Can of compressed air
>
> Soft, lint-free cloth (I use cut-up old T-shirts)
>
> Small screwdrivers
>
> Natural-bristle paintbrush (or the lint brush that came with your machine)
>
> Tube of sewing machine oil
>
> Tube of sewing machine lubricant
>
> Cotton swabs (for lint removal or lubricant/oil application)
>
> Tweezers

2   Unplug the machine and remove the thread and bobbin thread, then give the exterior a wipe-down with a cloth. Remove the throat plate and bobbin case as directed in your manual, and use compressed air and/or a paintbrush to loosen and remove lint from the machine's nooks and crannies. (Don't forget to remove lint from the thread guides, too.) If there's any thread or lint packed into tight areas, remove it with tweezers. Then, oil and lubricate the machine as indicated in your owner's manual—keeping in mind that some newer, computerized machines don't require oil. Keep your manual handy and follow the guidelines described therein.

Get Organized A three-ring binder is a super handy way to keep your patterns and appliqué templates organized. Get a binder, a box of plastic protector sleeves, and some separator tabs. Use the sleeves to stash your loose pattern pieces and such, using the separator tabs to divide them into categories, such as Clothing, Accessories, etc. You could also add a section for holding fabric swatches—just staple them to a thick sheet of paper and punch with a three-hole punch.

Change It Up Is your machine skipping stitches, causing thread to bunch, or just plain acting weird? Many times, this is all due to a dull needle. It's important to change out your sewing machine needle regularly, since a dull one won't pierce the fabric properly and may end up getting bent, which can damage your bobbin—not to mention the project you've been working so hard on. A good rule of thumb is to switch the needle out every 8 hours of sewing (or with every new project).

TIPS

✳ When you're done oiling your machine, grab some scrap fabric and stitch a bit on that before starting your next project. That way, if there's any excess oil hanging around, it will be absorbed on the scrap, not your "good" fabric.

✳ If you're using a vintage sewing machine or family hand-me down, chances are the manual has gone missing. E-Bay to the rescue! There are a ton of sellers offering photocopied or PDF versions of long out-of-print manuals, which can be a real lifesaver.

Chapter 1 Pretties

Pretties

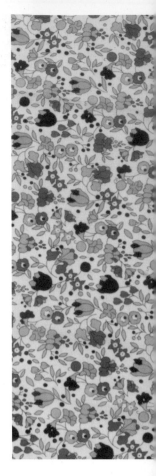

Expressing your individuality through your clothes and accessories can be as easy as picking up a needle and thread. This chapter will show you how to create some all-new wardrobe pieces, as well as how to use simple techniques to make over what you already have. Read on and discover how to use colorful topstitching to make yourself a tough-yet-girly cuff-style bracelet. Or pretty up a simple tank top with beading, embroidery, and appliqué to turn a wardrobe staple into a showpiece. Mix fabric colors and patterns when designing your own lightweight patchwork scarf, or stitch up a few fabric yo-yos and make a new necklace-and-earring set. Hide your overgrown bangs with a retro-sweet reversible headband, or craft a boutique-worthy cardigan by stitching on a pretty new collar and cuffs from recycled doilies.

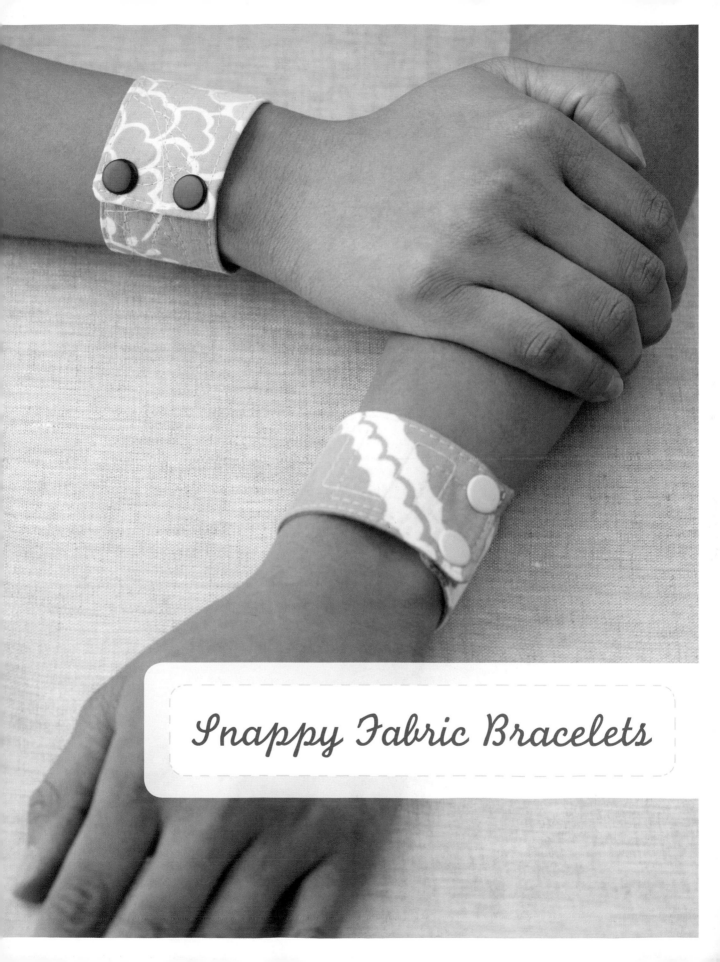

Snappy Fabric Bracelets

*Jewelry doesn't always have to be made from gemstones and precious metals—*it can also be made from fabric. These cuff-style bracelets are a breeze to whip up and can easily be made for dudes or dames, depending on what kind of fabric you use. Freestyle topstitching adds a personal touch, but feel free to further customize your bracelet by adding ribbons, buttons, or beads.

I like to use candy-colored snaps to close my bracelets, but you can use subtler sew-on snaps or even Velcro if you're so inclined. You could also add a special button and add a button-hole at one end of the bracelet.

Materials

3½" x 9" piece of floral cotton fabric

3½" x 9" piece of lightweight fusible interfacing

Two size 16 (⁷⁄₁₆") SnapSetter snaps (see Resources, page 141)

Coordinating and contrasting thread

Basic sewing tools (see page 15)

Prepare the Pieces

Iron the interfacing to the fabric.

Sew and Embellish

NOTE: *All seam allowances are ¼" unless otherwise noted.*

1   Fold the interfaced fabric in half lengthwise (long ends together) with the right sides together and pin the edges. Sew the two short edges and along the long open side, leaving a 2" opening along the side. Turn inside out and press flat.

MIX IT UP Using a different color of bobbin thread when you do the topstitching adds an extra punch of color with zero extra effort. Flip the bracelet over and sew to reverse the colors.

2   Topstitch all around the sides of the bracelet, ⅛" in from the edge. Stitch all over the rest of the bracelet with any decorative stitch pattern you like.

3   Attach the snaps to each end of the bracelet, as close to the corners as possible following manufacturer's instructions.

CUSTOM FIT This pattern makes a bracelet that fits wrists with a 7" circumference and smaller. They look great when worn close on the wrist like a cuff, or loose (like a bangle) on those of you with smaller wrists. Before you do the topstitching in step 2, wrap the bracelet around your wrist to see how it fits. It should go all the way around your wrist, overlapping by ½"–¾" to allow for snap placement. If you'd like it smaller, turn it wrong side out again and sew again on one end to create a tighter fit. Trim excess fabric, then turn right side out and press flat.

Necklace
Tank

Tank tops are an indispensable piece in every girl's wardrobe. They're cute, cheap, and available in a million colors—just the thing for layering with tiny cardigans, jean jackets, or even under a simple jumper-style dress. Here's a quick and easy way to turn the humble tank top into a sartorial superstar.

Using fabric scraps, embroidery floss, and a few beads or buttons, create a trompe l'oeil "necklace" around the collar of a plain tank top. It's a great way to use up odds and ends, and it only takes an hour or so to stitch up. Here I've used a variety of vintage and new cotton quilting fabrics in coordinating (but not "matchy-matchy") prints. Using gold or silver metallic embroidery floss to stitch the "chain" around the neckline gives it a subtle sparkle, but you can use any color you wish.

Materials

Ribbed cotton tank top (or non-ribbed, if you prefer)

Fabric scraps in 5 or 6 different patterns

HeatnBond Lite fusible adhesive

6 coordinating buttons or beads

Coordinating thread

Gold or silver metallic embroidery floss, and embroidery needle

Basic sewing tools (see page 15)

Prepare the Pieces

Following the manufacturer's instructions, iron the HeatnBond to the fabric scraps.

> **SIMPLIFY THE PROCESS** I prefer to fuse the HeatnBond to several large squares of fabric before drawing and cutting the oval shapes: It's much easier than matching up the shapes and ironing them after the fact. You can cut out enough shapes to make several tops at one time.

Draw 6 half-oval shapes on the HeatnBond side of the fabric scraps. The half-ovals should be no wider than 1¾" at their widest point, but feel free to experiment with the sizes. Cut out the shapes.

Sew and Embellish

NOTE: *All seam allowances are ¼" unless otherwise noted.*

1   Remove the adhesive backing from the HeatnBond. Arrange the half-oval shapes around the bottom edge of the tank top's neckline and iron in place.

2   Stitch along the rounded edge of each half-oval using a straight stitch, then stitch along the neckline edge of the half-ovals using a zigzag stitch.

3 Hand-stitch with a long running stitch (see page 19) around the neckline using metallic embroidery floss, leaving ¼" of the tank top's neckline showing between stitches and pushing the needle through only the top layer of neckline fabric (see below).

NO-SCRATCH STITCHES Metallic embroidery floss can be a little scratchy against bare skin, so as you're hand-stitching around the neckline, be sure to push the needle through only the outer layer of fabric. This is easier to do than you'd think, since a tank top's neckline is essentially a flattened tube.

4 Sew three buttons or beads on each side of the neckline, about ½" apart.

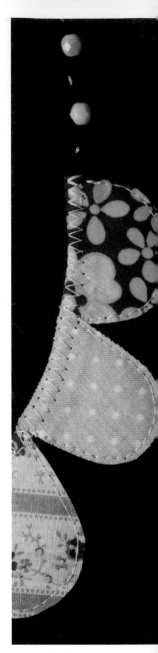

Themes and Variations

A great way to make use of fabric scraps, this simple "necklace" technique can be applied to all sorts of other garments. Here are just a few ideas.

- **Belted Tank** Instead of creating a "necklace" around the neckline of your tank, create a "belt" at the hem of your tank top consisting of 10 to 12 half-ovals from different fabric scraps for the front of the tank, and another 10 to 12 half-ovals if you want to circle the back, too.

- **Long Underwear Necklace Tee** Create a "necklace" around the neckline of a long-sleeve long underwear shirt. Choose soft flannel fabrics and skip the buttons in case you want to wear this tee to bed!

- **Garland Skirt** Use the same technique along the hemline of a skirt, adding embroidery stitches and beaded accents wherever the mood strikes you.

Fabric
Button
Necklace

When it comes to creating one-of-a-kind accessories, don't be afraid to look beyond the jewelry box. A growing number of crafters are finding inspiration in their sewing baskets, and I'm no exception. This necklace features simple fabric yo-yos and a variety of buttons (both fabric-covered and vintage plastic) stitched together and sewn onto a length of green wooden beads. The end result is eye-catching, organic-feeling, and entirely original.

I've designed this necklace to slip easily over your head, but if you have jewelry-making experience, you may choose to shorten the necklace to your liking using crimp beads and a lobster clasp instead.

Materials

Fabric scraps with small floral or novelty prints

2 fabric button blanks: 1 size 36 (⅞"), 1 size 60 (1½")

Small plastic, wooden, or glass button (approximately ¾")

Wooden beads (approximately ¼" diameter)

Waxed linen or cotton cord

Coordinating thread

Basic sewing tools (see page 15)

Fabric glue

Sew and Embellish

1 Sew three fabric yo-yos using the directions on page 16. Make one 2⅜" yo-yo, one 1¾" yo-yo, and one 1¼" yo-yo. Use a different fabric for each yo-yo.

2 Create two fabric buttons (see page 15), using a different fabric for each button, with the button blanks.

3 Sew the 1½" button to the center of the 2⅜" yo-yo, then the ⅞" button to the center of the 1¾" yo-yo. Finally, sew the ¾" button to the center of the 1¼" yo-yo.

4 Place the 1¾" yo-yo on the left side of the 2⅜" yo-yo, overlapping the edges by ¼" to ½". Stitch into place using coordinating thread, sewing from the underside of the yo-yos so as to hide your stitches.

5 Place the smallest yo-yo below the first two, overlapping by ¼" to ½". Stitch into place using coordinating thread, sewing from the underside of the yo-yos so as to hide your stitches.

6 Cut a length of waxed cord long enough to slip over your head, plus 6–7"; approximately 30" total. Tie a knot at one end leaving a 3" tail, and string wooden beads onto the cord until you have the necklace as long as you'd like it. Knot the ends together two or three times and snip off the excess cord. Dab the knot with a bit of fabric glue and allow to dry.

7 String a needle with a 20" length of thread and knot the ends together so you'll be sewing with a double thickness of thread. Place the yo-yos right side down and insert the needle and thread at the top left edge. Start attaching the strand of beads to the back of the yo-yos, hiding your stitches between each bead (and being careful not to push through to the front). Tie a double knot to end and snip off excess thread.

Themes and Variations

Don't limit yourself to making necklaces! You can make a jewelry box full of fabric-enhanced pretties using these simple variations.

- **Get an Earful** Cover two size 24 (⅝") button blanks with pretty fabric, then remove the shank loops with pliers. Glue two stud earring blanks to the back and voilà! Earrings to match your necklace.

- **A Must-Do** Stitch or glue a button-adorned yo-yo to a plain metal hairclip or bobby pin for an instant hairdo enhancer.

- **Pin One On** Stitch or glue a button-adorned yo-yo to a metal pinback to make a fresh and frilly brooch.

Skinny Scarf

Here in Los Angeles, I don't have much use for heavy woolen scarves, but on chillier-than-normal winter evenings I do like something warm around my neck, and in the summertime a scarf is just right for adding a bit of flair to an outfit. This long, skinny fabric scarf, made cozy with a thin layer of quilt batting, is lightweight enough to wear with a T-shirt or along with a cardigan or blazer in colder climates—try making it with panels cut from felted sweaters if you need extra warmth!

Finished Measurements

3½" x 67½"

Materials

Three 4" x 5½" green cotton
    fabric panels

Four 4" x 4½" fabric panels
    (2 green cotton, 2 natural-
    colored linen)

Seven 4" x 3½" fabric panels
    (1 green, 3 pink, and 2 lemon
    cotton; 1 natural-colored linen)

Five 4" x 2½" fabric panels
    (1 green, 1 lemon, and 1 pink
    cotton; 2 natural-colored linen)

Five 4" x 1½" fabric panels
    (3 lemon, 2 pink cotton)

4" x 68" piece of natural-colored
    linen for backing

4" x 68" piece of Warm &
    Natural cotton quilt batting

Coordinating and
    contrasting thread

Basic sewing tools (see page 15)

Sew and Embellish

NOTE: *All seam allowances are ¼" unless otherwise noted.*

1   Place any one of the fabric panels right side up at the bottom, short edge of the quilt batting.

2   Place a second panel on top of the first, right sides together, top edges aligned. Pin the panels in place and sew through all three layers (including the batting) along the top edge of the panels. Flip the second panel right side up and press flat.

3   Repeat step 2 with the additional panels, adding onto the strip and alternating colors however you prefer.

4   Place the long linen strip on top of the long strip of colored panels, right sides together, and pin in place. Starting in the middle of one long side, sew all around the edges, leaving an 8" opening for turning the scarf right side out. Trim any excess batting, then turn the scarf right side out and press flat.

5   Pin the opening closed and topstitch all around the edges of the scarf, ⅛" in from the edge.

6   Stitch directly over the seams between the fabric panels (see Stitch in the Ditch, opposite) using a variety of thread colors if you'd like. This looks especially pretty against the plain linen backing.

Tricks of the Trade

- **Piece It Together** You can piece together the linen backing to this scarf using several shorter pieces of linen sewn together to create one long, continuous strip.

- **Get a Handle on It** To keep the bulk manageable as you sew, you may find it helpful to roll up the ends of the scarf and pin the rolls to secure them.

- **Color Combos** I've suggested a palette of lemon, green, and pink paired with natural linen for this scarf, but the possibilities are endless. Another combo you might try: chocolate-colored linen with pink, cream, and caramel-colored fabric panels.

- **Shifty Business** Because batting tends to shift a bit as you sew it, the batting and linen backing are cut ½" longer than the strip of colored panels will end up. If any extra batting or backing hangs off the edge after you sew around the edge of the scarf, just trim it off before you turn the scarf inside out.

- **Stitch in the Ditch** The layers of this scarf are secured together with a quilting technique known as "stitching in the ditch." This simply means that you sew along the lines where the patchwork blocks meet. When you do this, your stitching will be invisible from the top but will show through on the linen backing. Remember to backstitch at the beginning and end of each row.

4-in-1
Reversible
Headband

Whether your hair is long or short, this headband is a fun way to tame your tresses while perking up your look. You can wear it with the bow at the nape of your neck or with the bow tied toward the front for a retro pin-up girl kind of vibe. There are two ways to wear it and two different fabric combinations, giving you four unique looks in one easy-to-make accessory.

Finished Measurements

2½" x 36"

Materials

7" x 22" piece of floral cotton fabric

7" x 22" piece of polka-dot cotton fabric

Coordinating thread

Basic sewing tools (see page 15)

Pattern Piece A (page 129)

Pattern Piece B (page 129)

Prepare the Pieces

Fold each piece of fabric in half (so the short ends are lined up) and press. Place the wider short edge of Pattern Piece A (the center section) on the fold on the floral fabric, then trace and cut through both layers with a rotary cutter. Repeat with the polka-dot fabric.

Trace and cut two of Pattern Piece B (the tapered ends) from the remaining floral fabric and two of Pattern Piece B from the polka-dot fabric.

Sew and Embellish

NOTE: *All seam allowances are ¼" unless otherwise noted.*

1   Place the Piece A sections right sides together and pin. Sew up both sides, leaving the short ends open, to create the center section. Turn right side out and press.

2   Place one floral and one polka-dot Piece B right sides together and pin. Sew up the curved sides, leaving the short end open, to create a tapered end. Turn right side out and press. Repeat with the second floral and polka-dot Piece Bs.

3   Fold the open ends of the center section inside about ¼" and press. Place floral side up. Insert the raw (open) edges of one tapered end, floral side up, into each opening about ¼" and pin in place.

4   Topstitch all around the four edges of the center section, ⅛" in from the edge, to secure the tapered ends in place.

GUSSY IT UP Feel free to embellish your headband with embroidery or ribbon—buttons would be fun, too! You could also keep the headband as is, and pin a glittery or flowery brooch to it for added pizzazz.

Customized Cardigan

Nothing beats a cardigan when it comes to adding a bit of warmth to your wardrobe or turning a ho-hum outfit into something special. With a few simple tweaks, you can turn a plain-Jane sweater into a one-of-a-kind creation that will have your fashionista friends turning green with envy. Better yet, you can use a sweater you already have (or a thrift store find) and recycled linens to make it on the cheap.

One thing to make sure of is that you choose a sweater with a tightly woven knit—otherwise, when you shorten the sleeves to that flattering ¾ length, the yarn may unravel. If you're at all uneasy about chopping up your sweater (or if you prefer the look of a longer sleeve) feel free to leave them as is and simply trim the ends with lace or ribbon.

Materials

Long-sleeved cardigan

2–3 embroidered table runners, doilies, or other old linens

Fabric-covered button blanks (see page 15)

Coordinating ribbons or lacy trims (for sleeve ends)

Package of wide single-fold bias tape or twill tape (optional)

Coordinating thread

Basic sewing tools (see page 15)

Prepare the Pieces

Wash and dry the sweater according to manufacturer's instructions. Wash, dry, and press linens. Using a seam ripper and/or small scissors, remove the sweater's original buttons.

Sew and Embellish

NOTE: *All seam allowances are ¼" unless otherwise noted.*

1   Try on the sweater, marking a spot or line on each sleeve approximately 4–5" above your wrists. Take off the sweater, laying it on a cutting mat. Flatten the sleeves, then cut off each sleeve end at the line you marked using a ruler and rotary cutter.

2   Choose one or two ribbons or trims to decorate your sleeve ends. Pin the trim into place starting at the sleeve's seam. Hand-stitch into place all the way around, being careful to position the trim so it covers the cut end of your sweater sleeve. When you reach the starting point, overlap the trim by ½" and snip with small scissors. Stitch the end down, tucking ¼" of the raw end underneath first.

3   If you choose to add a second trim to your sleeve (as shown), use a narrower trim and attach using the same method. Be sure to align this piece toward the top edge of the first trim you added, so that both trims will show, producing a layered look.

4   Lay the sweater on a cutting mat with the inside facing down so the neck and collar are flat (right side facing up). Begin experimenting with the linens, placing them along the top edge of the sweater to create a collar-like look, utilizing the existing edges of the pieces. Depending on the size and shape of your linens, you may end up using between two and three different pieces of fabric to make up your collar. My example uses three pieces total: one at the back of the neck and two on front (which overlap the back piece at the shoulders). The front parts of my collar measured about 4" (pre-sewing) and the back collar piece measured about 5½" (pre-sewing).

5   Once you know how you'd like to arrange your linen pieces along the neckline, mark a cutting line ½" out from the sweater's neck. The linen pieces used for the front of the sweater should also be cut ½" out from the sides of the button bands as well.

6   Pin the back collar piece into place, folding the additional ½" over the edge of the collar so the raw edges are on the inside of the sweater and the top edge of the sweater is covered. Sew the piece into place along all edges.

7   Place and pin the two front collar pieces, also folding the additional ½" over the edge of the collar so the raw edges are on the inside of the sweater. Sew along the neckline first, then fold the additional ½" over the button placket edges and pin into place. Sew down those edges and along the rest of the unattached edges.

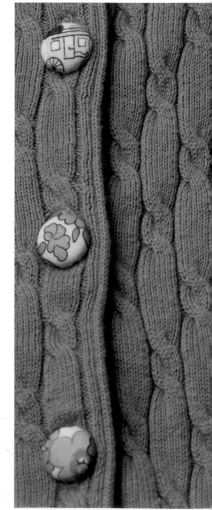

8   For a more professional look, you may wish to cover the raw collar edges on the inside of the neckline. To do so, cut a length of single-fold bias tape (or twill tape) that is 1" longer than your neckline. Lay the sweater down with the front facing up and the sides spread open and flat. Fold the tape over ½" at one end and pin into place at the inside left corner of the neckline. Hand-sew the starting edge into place, then pin the tape all along the neckline's top edge, covering anything you don't want visible. Whip-stitch into place along the top of the neckline with coordinating thread, stopping 1" before you reach the collar's end. Fold the tape under ½" and pin down at the inside right corner of the neckline, then hand-stitch into place. Finish up by whip-stitching the tape's bottom edge to the inside of the sweater, being careful not to push the needle all the way through to the outside.

9   Replace the buttons you've removed with the custom fabric buttons you've made (in a size similar to the sweater's original buttons) with the technique outlined on page 15. I prefer to use buttons in a variety of fabrics just to mix things up. You can do the same, or choose a more subtle approach. If your cardigan has buttons that go all the way up the sweater, you may need to cut a new buttonhole or two in the collar you've created. All you need to do is cut a slit in the collar fabric using a craft knife (using the old buttonhole as a placement guide) and use your sewing machine's buttonhole function to finish it off (see your machine's manual for instructions).

Themes and Variations

- ⊙ **Buttonpalooza** Instead of using fabric-covered buttons as closures, try using a multi-colored mix of vintage buttons.

- ⊙ **Garden Party** Sprinkle a hand-ful of fabric yo-yos (see page 16) around the collar, and stitch on a few small, green, leaf-shaped appliqués here and there for a floral effect.

- ⊙ **Sewing Circle** I used already-embroidered vintage linens on the neckline to get a chic look with zero extra effort. But if you're feeling extra crafty, you could of course add your own embroidered details.

Chapter 2 Totables

Totables

When I first started sewing, my main motivation was learning how to make my own bags. It may be a cliché, but I'm definitely addicted to cute bags—and the nice thing is, they're completely utilitarian, so there's always a way to justify buying yet another yard of special fabric for a tote-to-be. If you're an addict as well, this chapter is definitely for you. You'll learn to make a fun appliquéd eyeglasses cozy, complete with beaded accents—or create a simple tote adorned with playful sweet treats. Learn how to insert a zippered pocket with the Pillowcase Purse or in the kicky embroidered wristlet you can wear anywhere. Stash your beauty supplies in the Terrycloth Travel Pouch, which features a charm-festooned zipper pull—or make yourself a laptop bag that manages to do the impossible: look girly while protecting your computer.

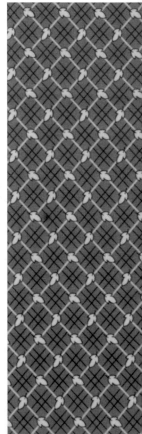

Eyeglasses
Cozy

Years of peering at a computer screen and embroidery hoop finally caught up with me, and last year I was forced to start wearing glasses. Rather than bemoan this fact, I embraced "geek-chic" and sought out the most stylish pair of vintage frames I could find—and now I love being called Four-Eyes. Those very frames were the inspiration for this appliquéd eyeglasses cozy, which I use to stash my precious specs when they're not in use.

Finished Measurements

3½" x 6¾"

Materials

¼ yard of chocolate brown linen or similar fabric (for exterior)

½ yard of patterned cotton fabric (for lining)

2¼" x 6" piece of felt (for eyeglass appliqué)

2¼" x 6" piece of patterned cotton fabric (for eyeglass appliqué)

Two 2¼" x 6" pieces of HeatnBond Lite fusible adhesive

¼ yard of Warm & Natural quilt batting

Pink, green, and red or other contrasting thread

Coordinating thread

5–6 metallic seed or crystal beads

Basic sewing tools (see page 15)

Pattern Piece A (page 129)

Pattern Piece B (page 129)

Prepare the Pieces

Exterior: Cut two 4½" x 7¾" rectangles from the linen exterior fabric and quilt batting. Mark out diagonal lines over the entire surface of the linen, about 1" apart (See Tape Tip, page 67). Place a linen rectangle on top of a quilt batting rectangle, marked side facing up, and pin layers together. Stitch layers together, sewing along diagonal lines using alternating colors of thread. Repeat for second piece of linen exterior fabric and quilt batting.

Patterned cotton lining fabric: Cut two 4½" x 7¾" rectangles each from the cotton lining fabric.

Appliqué: Fuse HeatnBond pieces to wrong side of felt and patterned cotton pieces. When cool, trace Pattern Piece A onto the paper side of the cotton fabric and cut out. Follow by tracing Pattern Piece B onto the paper side of the felt and cut out.

> **SPECS APPEAL** My cozy is quilted with multicolored thread and features a fun felt appliqué with hand-stitched beaded trim. You could customize your own cozy any number of ways, using sequins or rhinestones instead of beads, metallic thread for the diagonal stitching, or even vinyl for the eyeglass appliqué.

Sew and Embellish

NOTE: *All seam allowances are ¼" unless otherwise noted.*

1   Place one exterior piece right side up on an ironing board. Peel paper backing from Piece B and center on top, adhesive side down. Iron to fuse.

2   Peel paper backing from Piece A and center on top of Piece B, adhesive side down. Iron to fuse.

3   Topstitch around all edges of felt eyeglass frames using coordinating thread, sewing as close to the edge as possible. Hand-stitch a few beads in the corners of the eyeglass frames.

4   Place exterior pieces right sides together. Pin and sew along three sides, leaving the top edge open.

5   Place interior pieces right sides together. Pin and sew along three sides, leaving top edge open. Turn right side out.

6   Insert lining piece into the exterior of the cozy with right sides together, lining up the side seams and pinning those first to keep things symmetrical. Pin the lining and exterior pieces together at the top and sew, leaving a 2½" opening along one side for turning right side out.

7   Turn cozy right side out and press. Topstitch along top seam ⅛" from the edge using coordinating thread.

MADE IN THE SHADE This cozy is sized to fit an average pair of eyeglasses — but not to worry, it will accommodate your oversized Jackie O–style sunglasses, too.

Sweet Treat
Appliquéd
Tote

If you've never sewn a bag before, these simple totes are the perfect starter project for you. And although the bag itself is straightforward and uncomplicated to make, the confectionery-themed appliqué adorning the front will set your tote apart from the pack. Choose from three different appliqué templates I've created for you—cupcake, layer cake, or ice cream—or come up with your own! Incidentally, these totes are the perfect size for carrying around a stack of your favorite crafty magazines.

Finished Measurements

12" x 15"

Materials

½ yard of cotton corduroy or denim (for exterior)

½ yard of polka-dot cotton lining fabric (for lining)

Felt and fabric scraps (for appliqué)

½ yard of lightweight fusible interfacing

Two 26" lengths of cotton webbing for straps

HeatnBond Lite fusible adhesive

Coordinating thread

Embroidery floss in 2–3 colors and embroidery needle

Sew-in snap closure (optional)

Basic sewing tools (see page 15)

Appliqué templates (pages 130–131)

Prepare the Pieces

Corduroy exterior fabric: Iron the fusible interfacing to the wrong side of the corduroy and cut out two 12¾" x 15¾" rectangles for the exterior of the bag, then two 2½" x 12¾" interior reinforcement strips (see Stay Strong, page 53, for more on reinforcement strips).

Polka-dot lining fabric: Measure and cut two 12¾" x 15¾" rectangles for the interior of the bag.

Appliqué: Select fabric and felt scraps a bit larger than the appliqué shapes you'd like to use, then iron a piece of HeatnBond to the wrong side of each. When cool, trace the templates onto the paper side of the fabric (if you use the layer cake template, flip the template over and trace a backward version). Cut out using sharp scissors.

Sew and Embellish

NOTE: *All seam allowances are ¼" unless otherwise noted.*

1   Put one large corduroy piece right side up on an ironing board. Place the appliqué adhesive side down in the lower right area of the rectangle, and iron to fuse layers together. Iron the appliqué pieces in the order indicated on the template(s).

2   Topstitch around all edges of the appliqué using coordinating thread, sewing about ⅛" from the edge. Add a few "sprinkles" on the appliqué by making a few random stitches with embroidery floss in 2–3 different colors.

3   Mark a horizontal line on each lining piece 1¾" down from the top edge. Place a corduroy reinforcement strip (from Prepare the Pieces, above) on each main lining piece, right sides together, with the long top edge of the strip along the horizontal line. (A 1-3/4" band of the lining piece will be visible above the reinforcement strip.) Pin in place, then sew the top edge of the strips down. Flip the strips so wrongs sides are together and press flat. (See photo on page 53 for example of reinforcement strip in its final position.)

4   Place lining pieces right sides together, then pin and sew along the sides and bottom edge. Press the seams open, then turn right side out.

5   Place exterior pieces right sides together (appliqué toward the bottom), then pin and sew along sides and bottom edge. Press seams open.

6   Pin the straps in place, hanging down the inside of the corduroy exterior, about 7" apart, leaving ½" of webbing peeking above the top. Be sure to pin from the outside of the bag so you don't mistakenly sew the pins into your lining.

7   With right sides together, insert the lining into the corduroy exterior, lining up the side seams and pinning those first to keep things symmetrical. Pin the lining and exterior pieces together at the top of the bag, being sure to catch the corduroy reinforcement strip, and sew, leaving a 4" opening for turning the bag right side out.

8   Turn the bag right side out, then press the top seam flat. Topstitch around the top opening of the bag ⅛" in from the edge. Hand-sew a snap closure into the bag, if desired.

Tricks of the Trade

- **The Key to It All** Before you stitch up the lining pieces, insert a folded 3" length of ribbon (with the cut ends together and facing out) between the layers in the reinforcement strip area. This gives you a nice loop you can hang a set of keys on or hook a pair of sunglasses to. You can use this little trick with almost any bag you make, and it comes in very handy!

- **Stay Strong** I always add a reinforcement strip to the interior linings of my bags, usually made from a piece of the same fabric used for the exterior. Lining fabrics are traditionally more lightweight than the outside of the bag, so including this strip at the top edge of the lining helps give the entire bag a more structured and professional look. Without it, the straps will wear more heavily on the lining fabric, and the cut ends of the handles will show through the lining as well.

- **A Close Shave** You can safely wash and dry this bag (cool water, low heat), but over time the felt parts of the appliqué will get a bit fuzzy, as all felt does. Just use a battery-operated lint shaver (available at any department store) and a light touch to remove any unsightly pills.

Pillowcase
Purse

I love collecting vintage bed linens from the '60s and '70s. There's something about the playful patterns that looks retro and fresh at the same time. In addition to using them in the bedroom, it's also fun finding ways to integrate them into your wardrobe, as in this sweet Pillowcase Purse.

Colorful daisy-strewn fabric squares are sewn into a patchwork strip that brightens up the dark denim. Jumbo rickrack creates a cute scalloped edge and echoes the bag's rounded corners. Additional pillowcase fabric is used as the lining. The zippered interior pocket features yet another patterned fabric, making this purse a veritable cornucopia of color.

Finished Measurements

13" x 11"

Materials

½ yard dark denim exterior fabric

½ yard floral cotton lining fabric

Three 4½" x 6" pieces of varying floral cotton fabrics for accent squares

Two 6¾" x 9" pieces of floral cotton fabric for pocket

½ yard medium-weight fusible interfacing

Two 26" lengths of cotton webbing for straps

11¾" length of jumbo rickrack

7" zipper

Sew-in snap closure (optional)

Coordinating and contrasting thread

Basic sewing tools (see page 15)

Pattern Piece A (page 132)

Prepare the Pieces

Denim exterior fabric: Iron the fusible interfacing to the wrong side of the denim exterior fabric. Mark and then cut two pattern piece A (the main piece) and two strips 2½" x 13¾" for interior reinforcement strips (see Stay Strong, page 53, for more on reinforcement strips).

Floral cotton lining fabric: Mark and then cut two pattern piece A (the main piece).

Sew and Embellish

NOTE: *All seam allowances are ¼" unless otherwise noted.*

1   Place two accent squares right sides together and sew along one of the 6" edges using coordinating thread. Press the seam open. Place the third accent square on the bottom square, right sides together, and sew along the 6" edge. Press the seam open.

2   Mark a vertical line 8½" from the left of the front denim main piece and pin rickrack over it. Hand-stitch the rickrack in place down the center of the rickrack using coordinating thread.

3   Place the accent square strip right side down on the rickrack, aligning the right-most edge of the fabric to the right-most edge of the rickrack. Pin in place and sew, stitching as close to the center of the rickrack as possible, using coordinating thread. Flip the accent square strip over so it's right side up and press flat. Trim any excess so the strip is flush with the right edge of the denim piece.

4   Pin the accent strip to the denim piece, then topstitch along the left edge of the strip, ⅛" in from the seam using contrasting thread. Topstitch along either side of the seams between the accent squares, ⅛" in from the seams, using contrasting thread.

THREAD TIPS When topstitching the patchwork panel and bag open-ing, use bright, candy-colored thread for a bit of contrast. When sewing the exterior and lining fabrics together, use a coordinating thread that doesn't stand out too much so that when you turn the pieces right side out you get a nice clean look.

5   Place the two main pieces of the denim right sides together and pin them in place. Sew the bottom and side seams, leaving the top edge open. Cut two notches into each curved corner, then press the seams open.

6   Mark a horizontal line on the right side of each lining piece, 1¾" down from the top edge. Place a denim reinforcement strip (from Prepare the Pieces, page 55) on each lining piece, right sides together, with the long top edge of the strip along the horizontal line. Pin in place, then sew the top edge of the strips down. Flip the strips right side up and press flat.

7   Insert a zippered pocket into one of the main lining pieces (see page 17 for instructions).

8   Place the lining pieces right sides together and pin them in place. Sew the bottom and side seams, leaving the top edge open and being sure to catch the ends of the reinforcement strips in the side seams. Cut two notches into each curved corner, then press the seams open. Turn the lining inside out.

9   Pin the straps in place, hanging down the inside of the denim exterior, about 7" apart, leaving ½" of webbing peeking above the top. Be sure to pin from the outside of the bag so you don't mistakenly sew the pins into your lining.

10   With right sides together, insert the lining into the denim exterior, lining up the side seams and pinning those first to keep things symmetrical. Pin the lining and exterior pieces together at the top of the bag, being sure to catch the denim reinforcement strip, and sew, leaving a 4" opening for turning the bag inside out.

11   Turn the bag inside out, then press the top seam flat. Topstitch around the top opening of the bag, ⅛" in from the edge, using contrasting thread. Hand-sew a snap closure into the bag, if desired.

Themes and Variations

- **Make the Most of It** If you end up with more pillowcase scraps than you know what to do with, consider making some matching Snappy Fabric Bracelets (page 25) or a 4-in-1 Reversible Headband (page 38).

- **Linen Pillowcase Purse** Dark denim is the perfect backdrop for these fun pillowcase fabrics, but natural-colored linen would provide a nice contrast as well.

- **Cold-Weather Pillowcase Purse** Want to take this idea into the chilly months? Make your tote from corduroy and use flannel sheets for the accent pieces and lining.

- **Stitch It Up** For an extra-personal touch, add embroidered accents to the patchwork panels of the purse before sewing it up.

- **Petite Pillowcase Purse** To create a pint-sized purse for a little girl, cut out all the pieces at 50 percent of the original size. Stitch them up with an extra rickrack stripe or two for fun.

Merit Badge
Wristlet

Why is it that when you learn a new skill as an adult, nobody gives you a merit badge? If I'd received a merit badge after learning to drive at age thirty, I would have felt a whole lot cooler! Here's a fun wristlet purse you can sew up for yourself that serves as a great place to display your own little personalized merit badge. The example I've made celebrates the art of sewing, but you could easily sketch up a simple badge motif to celebrate whatever accomplishment you choose.

Finished Measurements

9" x 6"

Materials

¼ yard of cotton canvas or denim-type fabric (for exterior)

¼ yard of patterned cotton lining fabric (for lining)

Felt scraps in two different colors (for appliqué)

¼ yard of lightweight fusible interfacing

Two 26" lengths of cotton webbing for straps

HeatnBond Lite fusible adhesive

Rickrack trim

7" zipper

Coordinating thread

Embroidery floss in pink, red, and gray, and embroidery needle

Basic sewing tools (see page 15)

Pattern Piece A (page 133)

Appliqué Template (page 133)

Prepare the Pieces

Canvas exterior fabric: Iron the fusible interfacing to the wrong side of the canvas. Trace and cut two of Pattern Piece A for the exterior of the wristlet, then measure and cut one 3" x 10½" strip for the wrist strap.

Patterned cotton lining fabric: Trace and cut two of Pattern Piece A for the interior of the wristlet.

Merit Badge Appliqué: Select felt scraps that are a bit larger than the appliqué template, then iron a piece of HeatnBond to the wrong side(s) of each. When cool, trace the templates (treat the circle and the spool separately) onto the paper side of the fabric and cut out using sharp scissors.

Sew and Embellish

NOTE: *All seam allowances are ¼" unless otherwise noted.*

1   Fold the wrist strap piece in half with long edges together. Pin and sew along long edge, then turn right side out using a loop turner (see page 13). Press flat (with seam on edge) and topstitch along both long edges with coordinating thread, about ⅛" from edge. Cut a 10½" strip of rickrack trim and pin into place down the center of the strap, then sew down the center of the trim.

2   Choose one canvas Piece A to be the front of your wristlet, then place the circle template where indicated. Trace around the template using water- or air-soluble pen.

3   Cut a length of rickrack trim and hand-stitch it to the canvas to cover the circle you just traced. Peel the paper off the felt circle you cut out earlier, then place it adhesive side down on top of the rickrack circle and iron to fuse. (The felt circle should cover the interior edges of the rickrack so that only a scalloped edge peeks out.) Topstitch around the circle's edges with coordinating thread about ⅛" from the edge.

4   Peel the paper off the spool motif you cut out earlier, then place adhesive side down in center of the felt circle and iron to fuse. Topstitch around the edges of the felt motif with coordinating thread about ⅛" from the edge.

5   Hand-stitch around the circle's edge using embroidery floss and a running stitch (see page 19), about ⅛" in from the line you topstitched earlier. Add other details with embroidery floss where indicated on the template.

6   Place the canvas exterior piece with the merit badge right side up, then place the zipper at the top edge (zipper pull side down), with the zipper pull at the left edge.

7   Place one piece of lining fabric right side down on top of the canvas piece and zipper, pinning layers together at top edge. Using your machine's zipper foot, sew along the top edge.

8   Flip fabric so wrong sides are together and press flat.

9   Place the remaining canvas exterior piece right side up, then place the zipper at the top edge (zipper pull side down), with the zipper pull at the right edge.

10 Place the remaining piece of lining fabric right side down on top of the canvas piece and zipper, pinning layers together at top edge. Using your machine's zipper foot, sew along the top edge.

11 Flip fabrics from step 10 so all wrong sides are together and press flat.

12 Switch back to your normal presser foot. Topstitch exterior and lining fabrics together along each long side of zipper, sewing about ⅛" from the edge.

13 Place exterior pieces and lining pieces right sides together (like facing like) and pin around all edges. Fold the strap piece in half with short, raw edges together and rickrack facing out, and slip it between the canvas exterior layers, about 1" down from zipper. The strap should be slipped in on the zipper pull edge, with raw ends sticking out about 1". Pin into place.

14 Sew around all edges of the wristlet, beginning at the bottom edge of the lining. Leave a 3–4" opening at center bottom of the lining for turning right side out. Press seams open.

15 Press down the bottom corners of the lining and exterior so they form a flat triangle shape. Mark a line about 1" in from each corner, then sew over the line and snip the corners off.

16 Poke your fingers through the opening in the lining fabric and push the zipper pull over until the zipper opens all the way. Turn the wristlet right side out and press out any wrinkles. Hand-stitch the opening in the lining closed using a hidden stitch (see page 19), or simply sew the bottom seam opening closed on the machine using coordinating thread. (If you choose the latter method, sew using a ⅛" seam allowance.)

Themes and Variations

- **Not Just for Grown-Ups** Make this project for a kid in your life—the wristlet size is perfect for toting around a few essentials like bubble gum and hair ties. This would also make a great "first day of school" gift: just fill it with essentials like pencils and erasers, a calculator, and a small notepad or two.

- **Girl Gang** Make a set of Merit Badge Wristlets for everyone in your craft group. You can personalize each wristlet with the recipient's favorite craft, and/or use it to display badges you collect from fun events you attend together. The wristlets are also perfect to use when collecting money at a craft fair—wearing it on your wrist means your hands will be free to rearrange your merchandise and pack up your customers' purchases.

Terrycloth
Travel
Pouch

It might sound eccentric, but I'm a sucker for vintage towels. Terrycloth came in such bright, unique colors and patterns back in the '60s and '70s that there's a wave of crafters refashioning them into useful and beautiful items today. I've seen everything from stuffed bears to bikinis made with vintage terrycloth. Since vintage towels always remind me of summer holidays at the beach, I created this terrycloth travel pouch to use the next time I take a vacation. Because it's made from sturdy toweling fabric, the pouch can really take a beating—and if your shampoo leaks, it won't be the end of the world.

Finished Measurements

8½" x 7½"

Materials

¼ yard of terrycloth (for exterior)

¼ yard of patterned cotton lining fabric (for lining)

¼ yard of lightweight fusible interfacing

Two 8½" pieces of ribbon trim

One 7" zipper

Jump rings, any color

2–3 charms or beads

Coordinating thread

Basic sewing tools (see page 15)

Jewelry pliers (or other small pliers)

Pattern Piece A (page 133)

Prepare the Pieces

Terrycloth exterior fabric: Iron the fusible interfacing to the wrong side of the terrycloth, then trace and cut out two of Pattern Piece A for the exterior of the pouch.

Patterned cotton lining fabric: Trace and then cut two of Pattern Piece A for the interior of the pouch.

Sew and Embellish

NOTE: *All seam allowances are ¼" unless otherwise noted.*

1   Once the fabric is cool, pin and sew ribbon trim on the right side of both terrycloth exterior pieces, 1½" down from the top edge.

2   Place one terrycloth exterior piece right side up, then place the zipper (zipper pull side down) at the top edge, with the zipper pull at the left edge.

3   Place one piece of lining fabric right side down on top of the terrycloth piece and zipper, pinning layers together at the top edge. Using your machine's zipper foot, sew along the top edge.

4   Flip fabric so wrong sides are together and press flat.

5   Place the remaining terrycloth exterior piece right side up, then place the zipper at the top edge (zipper pull side down), with the zipper pull at the right edge.

6   Place the remaining piece of lining fabric right side down on top of the terrycloth piece and zipper, pinning layers together at the top edge. Using your machine's zipper foot, sew along the top edge.

7 Place exterior pieces and lining pieces right sides together (like facing like, lining up the ribbon trims as best you can) and pin around all edges. Sew around all edges of the pouch, beginning at the bottom edge of the lining. Leave a 3–4" opening at center bottom of the lining for turning right side out. Press seams open.

8 Press down the bottom corners of the lining and exterior so they form a flat triangle shape. Mark a line about 1" in from each corner, then sew over the line and snip the corners off.

9 Poke your fingers through the opening and push the zipper pull over until the zipper opens all the way. Turn the travel pouch right side out and press out any wrinkles. Hand-stitch the opening in the lining closed using a hidden stitch (see page 19), or simply sew the bottom seam opening closed on the machine using coordinating thread. (If you choose the latter method, sew using a ⅛" seam allowance.)

10 Attach 2–3 charms or beads to the zipper pull, using jewelry pliers and jump rings (see Attaching Charms, page 19). Alternatively, you could simply thread a short length of pretty ribbon through the zipper pull and tie it in a knot.

Themes and Variations

- **Slippery When Wet** If you'd like to create a truly waterproof travel pouch, use iron-on vinyl to coat your lining fabric before sewing it up. Just don't forget to use a non-stick (or walking) foot when you get to the stitching part or your work can bunch up and the sewing can go very awry.

- **Charmed, I'm Sure** Personalize your pouch further by choosing unique charms to adorn the zipper pull. I chose bright daisies and teardrop shapes to complement the floral terrycloth, but you might prefer to use tiny cowboy boots, a skull and crossbones, or even a cluster of your favorite buttons. For recommendations on where to find great charms, see Resources (page 141).

Ladylike Laptop Tote

I love that technology allows me to carry a super-awesome computer anywhere I want, but I don't love all the drab, boring, and just plain ugly laptop cases on the market. I wanted to carry something unique and pretty—something that looked more like a proper handbag than a briefcase or foam-encased portfolio. So I created the Ladylike Laptop Tote, which fits laptops between 13–15" and features sunny-looking vintage pillowcase fabrics paired with classic gray linen. The interior features a double layer of quilt batting to protect your precious laptop, while the scallop-trimmed strap snaps closed to keep it from slipping out. The whole thing is finished off with multicolored, button-trimmed fabric yo-yos for a girlish look that definitely stands out in a crowd.

Finished Measurements

14" x 11"

Materials

½ yard of gray linen or similar fabric (for exterior)

½ yard of patterned cotton lining fabric (for lining)

½ yard of Warm & Natural quilt batting

4 button-embellished fabric yo-yos (page 16)

17" length of rickrack trim

Sew-in snap closure

Coordinating thread

Basic sewing tools (see page 15)

Prepare the Pieces

Exterior of bag: Cut two 11¾" x 16½" rectangles each from the linen exterior fabric and quilt batting. Mark out diagonal lines over the entire surface of the linen about 1" apart. Place a linen rectangle on top of a quilt batting rectangle, marked side facing up, and pin layers together. Stitch layers together, sewing along diagonal lines using coordinating thread. Repeat for second piece of linen exterior fabric and quilt batting.

Patterned cotton lining fabric: Cut two 11¾" x 16½" rectangles each from the cotton lining fabric and quilt batting. Mark out diagonal lines over the entire surface of the lining fabric, about 1" apart. Place a lining fabric rectangle on top of a quilt batting rectangle, marked side facing up, and pin layers together. Stitch layers together, sewing along diagonal lines using coordinating thread. Repeat for second piece of lining fabric and quilt batting.

TAPE TIP When marking out the diagonal lines for quilting your bag, you can do it with a ruler and some chalk, but I prefer using scotch tape! It's easy to use, is the ideal width, and lifts off leaving no residue. (The "Magic" kind is good because it's less sticky.) Just start by laying down a strip of tape on your fabric that runs diagonally from corner to corner. Working from either side of this first line, keep laying down strips of tape, aligning them the same way. Leave a strip of exposed fabric between each strip of tape approximately the same width (more or less) as the tape. Once the fabric is all covered, pin the fabric to the quilt batting and stitch the layers together, sewing on either side of the tape (but not through the tape). When it's all stitched up, remove the tape and marvel at your perfect stitching!

Closure flap: Cut one 4¼" x 6" rectangle from the linen exterior fabric, the quilt batting, and the cotton lining fabric. Mark out diagonal lines over the entire surface of the linen, about 1" apart. Place the linen rectangle on top of the quilt batting rectangle, marked side facing up, and pin layers together. Stitch layers together, sewing along diagonal lines using coordinating thread. Pin the rickrack around three edges of the linen piece (two long, one short), then place and pin cotton lining fabric piece right side down on the linen piece. Sew along the pinned edges, leaving the rickrack-free edge open. Remove pins, turn flap right side out, and press. Topstitch along the rickrack-trimmed edges of the flap about ⅛" from the seam.

Straps: Cut one 7" x 17" rectangle from the cotton lining fabric and fusible interfacing. Iron the interfacing to the wrong side of the lining fabric according to manufacturer's directions, then cut the rectangle in half to create two 3½" x 17" strips. Fold each strip in half lengthwise, right sides together. Pin and sew along the long edge, then turn right side out using a loop turner (see page 13). Press flat (with seam on edge) and topstitch along both long edges with coordinating thread, about ⅛" from the edge.

Sew and Embellish

NOTE: *All seam allowances are ¼" unless otherwise noted.*

1   Place linen exterior pieces right sides together and pin around left, right, and bottom edges. Sew along all pinned edges. Remove pins and press seams open.

2   Place cotton lining pieces right sides together and pin around left, right, and bottom edges. Sew along all pinned edges. Remove pins and press seams open.

3   Press down the bottom corners of the lining and exterior so they form a flat triangle shape. Mark a line about 1" in from each corner, then sew over the line and snip the corners off.

4   Pin the straps in place, hanging down the inside of the linen exterior piece, about 6" apart, leaving ½" of the strap ends peeking above the top. Be sure to pin from the outside of the bag so you don't mistakenly sew the pins into your lining.

5   Pin the closure flap in place between two of the straps, hanging down inside the linen exterior piece, with linen sides facing. Leave about ½" of the flap's raw edge peeking above the top.

6   Turn lining piece right side out, then insert into the exterior of the bag with right sides together, lining up the side seams and pinning those first to keep things symmetrical. Pin the lining and exterior pieces together at the top of the bag, and sew, leaving a 4" opening between the straps for turning the bag right side out.

7 Turn the bag right side out, then press the top seam flat. Topstitch around the top opening of the bag, ⅛" in from the edge. Hand-sew a snap closure to the flap and front of the bag.

8 Hand-stitch four yo-yos to the front of the bag, about 2½" below the flap. Use thread that coordinates with the yo-yos and keep your stitches as small as possible so they don't show too much.

MAKE IT A MAN PURSE I came up with this bag because I was looking for something frilly to tote around—but you could easily adapt the instructions to make a boyish (or gender-neutral) version. Just skip the yo-yos and rickrack, and use a solid denim or canvas fabric (something in a chocolate brown would look cool) for the exterior. You could use a solid-colored fabric for the lining, or perhaps a simple plaid or stripe pattern.

Chapter 3 Nest

Nest

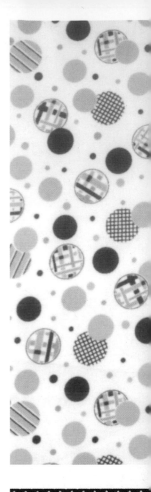

When decorating your home, the best thing you can do is surround yourself with items that have some kind of personal meaning—these little touches are exactly the thing that make a house a home. In this chapter, you'll learn how to make six such items, and you'll pick up some new skills in the process. Turn a pair of old curtains into a set of coasters stitched up with curlicues, or use simple appliqué techniques to give your kitchen window a whole new view. Perk up your dining room with a checkerboard table runner made from a salvaged tablecloth, or learn the basics of patchwork quilting while whipping up a comfy neck pillow. Finally, you'll dress your nest with a multi-layered fabric collage using those crafty odds and ends you aren't sure what to do with.

Recycled Coasters

I have a bad habit of repainting my living room every few years. I can't resist—there are too many great colors available to settle on just one! I've tried pale blue, sunny orange, and chocolate brown, and each time, I swap out the couch pillows, curtains, and other fabric accessories to match. I've discovered that making a set of fabric coasters is one of the quickest and easiest ways to tie together a new color scheme and round out a room's look. The Recycled Coasters were made using some '50s-era barkcloth curtains I bought at a flea market, with dark denim as a backing fabric. They feature free-motion quilting on top, which gives them a whimsical, casual look.

Finished Measurements

Approximately 4¾" x 4¾"

Materials

10½" x 10½" piece of barkcloth or any cotton fabric for top

10½" x 10½" piece of dark denim or similar weight fabric for bottom

10½" x 10½" piece of Warm & Natural quilt batting

Contrasting thread

Basic sewing tools (see page 15)

Sew and Embellish

NOTE: *All seam allowances are ¼" unless otherwise noted.*

1   Place the barkcloth right side up on top of the quilt batting and put both layers inside an embroidery hoop or secure the edges with safety pins. Topstitch a swirly design all over the fabric using the free-motion technique (see Embellishing Basics, page 16). Use a contrasting thread so it stands out.

2   Remove fabric from the embroidery hoop or remove the safety pins and press. Using a rotary cutter, cut the fabric down the middle horizontally and vertically, to create four 5¼" squares.

3   Using a rotary cutter, cut the denim down the middle horizontally and vertically, to create four 5¼" squares. Place each denim square and barkcloth square right sides together and pin.

4   Sew around all edges of each square, starting on the edge of one side and leaving a 2" opening for turning right side out. Once all squares are sewn, turn right side out and press.

5   Topstitch around all edges of each square (barkcloth side up), sewing about ⅛" from the edge. If desired, use a darker bobbin thread so it blends in with the denim.

Themes and Variations

- **Be a Square** Instead of topstitching loop-de-loop patterns, embellish the fabric with straight lines and sharp corners for a modern, geometric look.

- **Dye Job** If you use dark denim for the underside of your coasters, make sure to pre-wash it! The last thing you want is for indigo dye to stain your tables if it gets wet.

- **Be My Guest** Before you visit friends for the weekend, whip up a set of these coasters (ideally color coordinated with *their* living room) to give as a gift. You'll earn instant brownie points and will henceforth be known as their favorite houseguest ever.

Nice View
Café Curtain

Although I'd love to live in a quaint cottage somewhere, I live in an urban apartment building. This means that when I stand at the sink to wash dishes, I get an eyeful of whatever my neighbors are doing (whether I want to or not!). So I decided to create a café curtain for the kitchen window that would provide the kind of view I wish I had. The curtain itself is made from cotton eyelet fabric that lets plenty of light shine through, and the appliqués were created with linen and some colorful fabric scraps I had lying around. I love how the curtain looks in my colorful kitchen, but it would be equally cute hanging in a kid's bedroom.

Finished Measurements

20" x 26" (see tip on page 78 for customizing)

Materials

26" x 28" piece of white cotton eyelet fabric

Natural-colored linen, at least 9" x 12"

Green patterned fabric, 9" x 20" or smaller

Pink, red, and blue fabric scraps (for appliqué templates)

HeatnBond Lite fusible adhesive

Assortment of buttons and trims

White thread and thread that coordinates with the appliqué

Embroidery floss in green and pink and embroidery needle

Basic sewing tools (see page 15)

Appliqué templates (page 134)

Tension rod to fit your window

Prepare the Pieces

Select fabric scraps a bit larger than the appliqué template(s) you'd like to use, then iron a piece of HeatnBond to the wrong side(s) of each. When cool, trace the templates onto the paper side of the fabric. Cut out using sharp scissors.

Sew and Embellish

NOTE: *All seam allowances are ¼" unless otherwise noted.*

1   Turn one of the 26" edges of the cotton eyelet fabric over ½" and press. Turn over again ½", press and pin. Stitch along pressed side with white thread, sewing about ¼" from edge. Repeat on the other 26" edge.

2   Turn one of the 28" edges over ½" and press. Turn over again ½", press and pin. Stitch along pressed side with white thread, sewing about ¼" from edge.

3   Turn the other 28" edge over ¼" and press. Turn over another ¼" and press, then fold edge over 2" and press. Pin and sew edge of fold, sewing about ⅛" from edge. This opening is the sleeve for the curtain's tension rod.

4   Add a running stitch (see page 19) along the edge of the 2" fold using pink embroidery floss, then add another row of pink stitching along the bottom edge of the curtain.

5   Place a press cloth (a pillowcase will do fine) on an ironing board and place the curtain right side up on top. Remove the paper backing and iron on the appliqué pieces in the order indicated on the template(s).

6   Topstitch around all edges of each appliqué using coordinating thread, sewing about ¼" in from the edge. Add a line of stitching down the middle of each window horizontally and vertically.

7   Hand-sew a few buttons (to represent flowers) on top of the grassy hill, then add stems and leaves with green embroidery floss. Add a few more button flowers and stems on either side of the house's front door. If desired, add one more button to represent a doorknob.

8   Hand-stitch a bit of trim above the chimney to represent a plume of smoke, then insert the tension rod in the top sleeve pocket and hang.

Themes and Variations

- **Measuring Up** Remember that a cafe curtain only covers the bottom half of your window, which is why it's wider than it is tall. My curtain fits just right in my window, which is about 22" wide. I intentionally created a curtain that didn't have much volume, so the countryside scene would read clearly. To customize this curtain to fit your window, follow this formula: 1) Measure half the window's height, add 4" to allow for hemming and rod pocket, 2) measure the window's width, and add 6" for side hems and a bit of volume. (For a fuller-looking curtain, add up to 14" to the width.)

- **Kid Stuff** I wanted the art on this curtain to look simple and childlike, like a drawing you'd pin on the fridge. If you have access to real, live, pint-sized Picassos, invite them to help decorate the curtain with flowers, animals, or whatever else strikes their fancy.

- **City House, Country House** I designed a curtain that would get my mind off city living—but if you're in the country and yearn for the opposite, you could cut out some fabric rectangles in varying widths and heights and create a whimsical cityscape instead.

Checkerboard Table Runner

MATCHING NAPKINS If you have any tablecloth scraps left over after sewing the table runner, stitch up a set of napkins to match. Cut scraps into 11" x 11" squares, then fold (toward the wrong side of fabric) and press each edge over by ¼". Fold and press edges by ¼" again and sew around all edges, stitching about ⅛" from the edge.

I'm an avid collector of '50s-era tablecloths, but it can be such a bummer when I find one with a gorgeous pattern and vibrant colors—and too many set-in stains to ever use. I've decided there's no sense in letting such pretty designs go to waste, though, so I find other ways to use them—like in this checkerboard table runner. Here I've cut the prettiest sections from a damaged tablecloth and stitched them together with some chocolate-colored linen to create a table runner that's elegant enough for company, yet casual enough to leave on the table 24–7.

Finished Measurements

15" x 67½"

Materials

Nine 8" x 8" pieces of cotton tablecloth fabric

Nine 8" x 8" pieces of linen or similar weight solid-colored fabric

15½" x 68" piece of linen of similar weight solid-colored fabric

Coordinating thread

Basic sewing tools (see page 15)

BACK IT RIGHT
Depending on the tablecloth fabric you use, you may want to choose a light-colored fabric for the underside of your table runner—a dark fabric may show through.

Sew and Embellish

NOTE: *All seam allowances are ¼" unless otherwise noted.*

1   Place one tablecloth square and one linen square right sides together. Pin along one edge and sew, then press seams flat. Repeat with remaining sixteen squares, making nine pairs.

2   Take one set of squares and place right side up. Place a second set of squares right side down on top of the first set, alternating the squares so opposite fabrics are facing one another. Pin along one long edge and sew, then press seam flat. Repeat with remaining seven sets of squares, continuing to alternate the placement of the squares.

3   Place the table runner right side up and top with the 15½" x 68" piece of linen. Pin and sew along all edges, leaving a 4" opening for turning right side out.

4   Turn right side out and press, then topstitch around all edges of the table runner, sewing about ⅛" from the edge. Sew all layers together, starting by stitching in the ditch (see Tricks of the Trade on page 37) along the center seams and continuing until all seams are stitched through.

Happy Hostess Dishtowels

SIZING TIP The dishtowel I used measures 16" x 26", but yours may be a different size. The vertical measurement of your fabric panel can stay the same, but you'll need to adjust the horizontal measurement so the panel is ½" wider than your particular towel. The same goes for the pieces of rickrack.

I believe that you can never have too many dishtowels. I keep a basketful in my kitchen, neatly folded and at the ready for a myriad of uses: catching spills, protecting my hands from hot pans, and just plain prettying up the joint. My favorite kind of towel is terrycloth, since they're so absorbent, but they can be a little on the boring side. Luckily, all it takes is a bit of fabric and some trim to turn a plain pair of dishtowels into charmingly retro kitchen accessories.

Materials

Terrycloth dishtowel

3½" x 16½" piece of patterned cotton fabric

Two 16½" pieces of rickrack trim

2½ yards of extra-wide double-fold bias tape (to make your own see page 18)

Coordinating and contrasting thread

Basic sewing tools (see page 15)

Sew and Embellish

NOTE: *All seam allowances are ¼" unless otherwise noted.*

1 Pin a length of rickrack trim about 3½" up from the bottom front edge of the dishtowel, folding the ends toward the back of the towel by ¼." Sew trim to towel, stitching down the middle of the rickrack with coordinating thread.

2 Repeat step 1, pinning the second length of rickrack 3" above the first one.

3 Place the strip of cotton fabric right side down, then fold both long edges over ¼" and press.

4 Place the strip of cotton fabric right side up on top of the rickrack, aligning it so the rickrack peeks out from behind the fabric strip. Pin into place and stitch along both edges, sewing about ⅛" from the edge.

5 Add six or seven more rows of stitching across the fabric panel, switching out the thread colors at least twice.

6 Attach the bias tape around the entire towel according to the directions on page 18, mitering the corners as described.

Themes and Variations

- **Mix It Up** Instead of using a single panel of fabric to decorate the dishtowel, you could create a strip of patchwork squares instead—or use free-motion topstitching instead of the straight stitching.

- **Gift It** The next time you need to give someone a housewarming gift, make a pair of dishtowels and tie them up with a length of ribbon. Add a set of measuring spoons or a set of blank recipe cards for a practical gift that will be used again and again.

Patchwork
Travel Pillow

I love visiting new places, but the flying part? Not so much. Being trapped on a plane for hours is rarely fun, but it can be a lot more comfortable if you come prepared. Dress in light layers, bring headphones or a good book, and make sure to bring your own pillow. This colorful patchwork pillow will provide your neck and head with the support you need to sleep, and the breathable cotton fabrics will leave you relaxed and ready for whatever your destination has in store. The comforts of this pillow aren't restricted to the friendly skies, either—bring one along on your next family trip and you can catnap on the go.

Finished Measurements

Approximately 11" x 12"

Materials

Assorted cotton fabric scraps, any variety of sizes, enough to cover Pattern Piece A

15" x 15" piece of cotton chenille

15" x 15" piece of Warm & Natural quilt batting

Nature-Fil Bamboo Fiber (or Poly-Fil) stuffing

Pattern Piece A (page 135)

Coordinating and contrasting thread

Basic sewing tools (see page 15)

Sew and Embellish

NOTE: *All seam allowances are ¼" unless otherwise noted.*

1   Choose a fabric scrap (piece 1) and place it right side up in the middle of the quilt batting. Place a second scrap (piece 2) right side down atop the first piece, aligning two of the edges along one side. Using coordinating thread, sew through all layers along the aligned side.

2   Flip piece 2 so it's right side up and press seam open. Trim raw edges of piece 2 so they line up with the edges of piece 1. Place a third fabric scrap (piece 3) right side down over pieces 1 and 2, aligning one edge along one of the raw edges of pieces 1 and 2. Sew through all layers along the aligned side.

3   Flip piece 3 so it's right side up and press seam open. Repeat steps 1–3 with remaining fabric pieces, working from the middle outward, until all of the quilt batting is covered.

Themes and Variations

- **Aromatherapy to Go** Sprinkle a handful of dried lavender buds into the stuffing of your pillow before you sew it closed. The herbal fragrance will help keep you mellow throughout any kind of turbulence.

- **A Touch of Home** When you're creating the patchwork part of your pillow, use fabrics snipped from your significant other's old clothes. Reminders of what you've got waiting back home can make traveling a whole lot easier.

4   Using a contrasting color of thread, topstitch along either side of the seams in the patchwork, sewing about ⅛" from the seam.

5   Place Pattern Piece A on top of the patchwork piece, trace, and cut out.

6   Place Pattern Piece A on the wrong side of the cotton chenille and trace. (It's easier than tracing on the right side, which is fuzzy.) Cut out and pin to the patchwork piece, right sides together.

7   Sew around all edges of the pillow, leaving a 3" opening for turning right side out.

8   Turn the pillow right side out and press. Fill with stuffing, then stitch opening closed using a hidden stitch (see page 19).

Apple Tree Fabric Collage

Appliqué isn't just for bags and clothes, and collages don't have to be made from paper—you can also create highly personalized works of art from fabric and thread. This fabric collage combines appliqué and embroidery with quirky embellishments like doilies, fabric yo-yos, and vintage buttons. Create your own using the apple tree stencil provided on page 136 and whatever craft supplies you have on hand. Use solid-colored fabrics and simple buttons for a minimal look, or go for broke with an exuberant mixture of patterns and textures.

Finished Measurements

8" x 10"

Materials

8" x 10" piece of solid cotton fabric (as a base)

8" x 10" piece of patterned cotton fabric

Felt and fabric scraps, various sizes

HeatnBond Lite fusible adhesive

Assortment of buttons, ribbons, and trim

Doilies, fabric yo-yos, and other embellishments as desired

Embroidery floss in various colors and embroidery needle

Basic sewing tools (see page 15)

Appliqué templates (page 136)

8" x 10" picture frame

Prepare the Pieces

Iron HeatnBond to the wrong side of the patterned cotton fabric and let cool. Peel off paper backing, then place adhesive side down onto solid cotton fabric. Iron to fuse.

Select fabric and felt scraps a bit larger than the appliqué template or shape you'd like to use, then iron a piece of HeatnBond to the wrong side(s) of each (treat the trunk and leaves separately). When cool, trace the templates onto the paper side of the fabric and cut out using sharp scissors.

Sew and Embellish

NOTE: *All seam allowances are ¼" unless otherwise noted.*

1   Peel the paper backing off each template piece and place adhesive side down in the center of the patterned cotton fabric. Iron down the tree trunk first, then the leaves.

2   Stitch around all edges of the tree using a running stitch (see page 19) and embroidery floss.

3   Add on whatever other accessories you like, stitching by hand or machine—see Themes and Variations, opposite, for tips.

4   Remove the glass from the picture frame and replace with your new fabric collage.

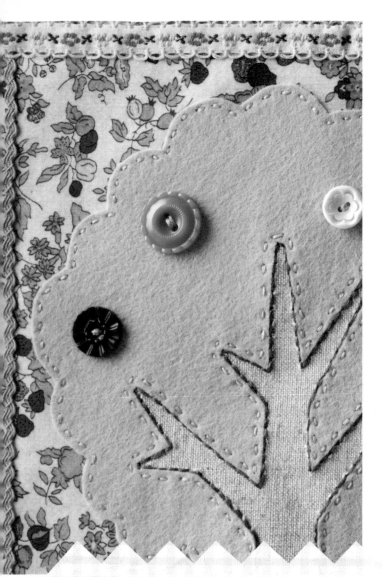

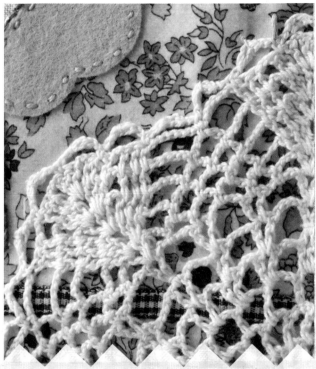

Themes and Variations

- **Make It Your Own** Although this project starts off with a simple apple tree template, the way you decorate it is entirely up to you. I used natural linen for the trunk of my tree to give it an earthy look, and I combined it with pale blue felt for the leaves of the tree. You might use bright green felt, or a rust color for an autumnal look. You could also use a patterned fabric for the trunk or leaves—the possibilities are endless.

- **Button Up** Button accents can be added to the tree as apple stand-ins, or you might use tiny fabric yo-yos instead. You might find a bird-shaped button and stitch that on, or maybe you'd like to try your hand at embroidering one amongst the leaves.

- **Improv Techniques** Ribbons can be used to border your piece, or you might add doilies and lace here and there. Once your tree is in place, pull out your sewing basket and spend some time adding and subtracting decorative elements like these until they're just the way you like them—then pull out needle and thread and affix them permanently.

Chapter 4 Kid Stuff

Kid Stuff

All too often, kids are barraged with cheesy, overly branded clothes and toys that say more about the company that made them (or the movie they're advertising) than they do about the wearer. This chapter aims to provide an antidote to all that, with a selection of fun yet sweet projects that will be a hit with parents and kids alike. Give a new mom an easy monogrammed onesie, or stitch up an offbeat teddy bear decorated with colorful fabrics and trims. Help keep mealtime tidy (well, as tidy as possible!) with a wipe-clean vinylized fabric bib, or use a stash of felted wool sweaters to sew up an extra-long and snuggly stuffed snake. Practice new quilting methods while making a teeny-tiny doll quilt, then graduate to the big leagues and sew a crib-sized beauty in subtle, confectionary-inspired colors.

Monogrammed
Baby Tee or Onesie

It seems as if everyone I know has either just had a baby or will be having one soon—which means I've got a lot of shower gifts to get ready! These sweet monogrammed baby tees and onesies fit the bill perfectly and are quick and easy to make. If you know the baby's name, you can customize it with their initial. If not, a set of three tees reading A, B, and C would be a fun alphabet-themed gift. You could also bypass the monogram idea entirely and adorn your onesie with freeform shapes or funny animal cutouts.

Materials

Baby T-shirt or onesie

Fabric scraps in various prints, at least 5" x 5"

HeatnBond Lite fusible adhesive

Baby rickrack trim and contrasting thread (optional)

Coordinating thread

Basic sewing tools (see page 15)

Printer or copier machine

Cardstock

X-Acto knife

Pencil

Create a Template

Using a computer program like Word or Photoshop, find a font you like (I used American Typewriter Bold) and print out a letter in black ink on cardstock. The letter should measure about 5" high. (Alternatively, you could hand-draw a letter on cardstock, or find a letter you like in a book and blow it up on a copier.) Use an X-Acto knife to cut out the letter; recycle the remaining cardstock.

Prepare the Pieces

Choose a piece of fabric and iron the HeatnBond to the wrong side according to manufacturer's directions. The piece of fabric you use should be large enough to fit your letter template.

Sew and Embellish

1   Once cool, flip the fabric so the paper side is facing up. Place the letter template right side down (so it reads backward) and trace with pencil. Cut out with sharp scissors. Small scissors can be especially helpful when cutting out detail areas.

2   Insert a press cloth (I use a folded floursack kitchen towel) between the front and back layers of your baby tee or onesie and lay it flat on an ironing board. Peel the paper from your cut-out letter and place right side up wherever you like on the tee. Iron together to fuse.

3   Once cool, remove the press cloth and machine-stitch the letter to the tee, sewing about ⅛" from the edges of the letter.

4   If desired, hand-sew trim to the neckline (see Trim It, opposite).

Themes and Variations

- **Trim It** Adding a bit of trim at the neckline gives the tee an extra pop of color (and looks just plain cute). Baby tees and onesies feature overlapping necklines, so you only want to add trim to the front part—otherwise the collar won't have enough stretch to fit over baby's head. In the example, I whip-stitched a scrap of baby rickrack to the collar using contrasting thread. The overlapping collar comes in handy, since it hides the beginning and ending of the trim.

- **Family Matters** Using the same appliqué technique, make a set of matching tees for mom and baby. Big brothers and sisters would probably love a shirt, too.

- **Keep It Safe** Instead of using your sewing machine to stitch down the appliqué, hand-sew with a running stitch (see page 19) and embroidery floss. Just be sure to use small, evenly spaced stitching to ensure that baby can't pull anything loose. A dab of fabric glue on the knots inside the tee couldn't hurt either.

Silly Snake

Usually, putting a wool sweater into a hot washing machine is a surefire recipe for tears and recriminations. But in the case of this fun project, it's cause for celebration! Using fuzzy felted sweaters gives this kooky stuffed snake toy an ultra-cozy look and feel. Felted wool is also easy to work with, since it doesn't fray when you cut it. Clocking in at more than four feet long, Silly Snake makes a snuggly bedtime companion and could also be used as a colorful draft stopper on cold winter nights.

Finished Measurements

Approximately 52" long x 6" wide

Materials

Assortment of felted sweaters
    (I used 8 to make my snake),
    from which you will cut:

* 1 of Pattern Piece A
    (head, page 137)
* 10 of Pattern Piece B
    (body, page 137)
* 1 of Pattern Piece C
    (tail, page 138)
* 2 of Pattern Piece D
    (mouth, page 138)
* 1" x 6" strip (tongue)

2–4 buttons for eyes (I used two
    stacked together for each eye)

Coordinating thread

Embroidery floss in coordinating
    colors and embroidery needle

Basic sewing tools (see page 15)

Beanbag filling
    (see Resources, page 141)

Sew and Embellish

NOTE: *All seam allowances are ¼" unless otherwise noted.*

1   Place the scalloped edge of one Piece B over the straight edge of Piece C, overlapping by about ½". Pin into place and topstitch along the scalloped edge, sewing about ⅛" from the edge.

2   Repeat step 1 with the nine remaining Piece B panels, adding onto the strip and alternating colors however you prefer. Finish by repeating step 1 with Piece A.

3   Flip the snake so wrong side is facing up, then trim off extra fabric where each layer is joined together, following the scallop-shaped stitching.

4   Fold the snake so the long, straight sides are together, pin into place, and sew, leaving the mouth end open. Turn the snake right side out.

5   Flatten the mouth and pin one Piece D to the right side of the snake's mouth, curved edges together. Sew along the curved edges of the mouth. Repeat on the other side of the mouth. Fold both sides of the mouth in so that their straight edges meet up inside the snake's mouth.

6   Slip the tongue into the snake's mouth and hand-sew to the center bottom of the mouth.

7   Mark two spots for the eyes, and hand-sew the buttons in place over them using embroidery floss.

8   Fill the snake's body with beanbag filling (using a funnel made from a piece of cardstock works well) until full. Hand-stitch the mouth opening closed using coordinating thread.

HOT FUZZ When you agitate a sweater made with at least 50 percent animal fiber (wool, alpaca, cashmere, etc.) in a hot washing machine with a bit of soap, it mats the fibers together and shrinks it up into a nice, tight felt that you can use to craft with. Tossing it in the dryer afterward can help shrink it up even more. It's a good idea to cut the sweater into pieces before washing (separate the arms from the body and front from the back) and—if you plan to felt a bunch of sweaters at once—combine like colors so if they bleed nothing is ruined.

Square Bear

Every kid needs a teddy bear, and this one definitely stands out from the crowd.
Inspired by Japanese comic books and my vintage button collection, Square Bear is a fun introduction to making stuffed animals. He's also very easy to customize, by mixing up the fabrics and trims you use. This bear is a great way to use up leftover fabric scraps from projects past and would make a seriously impressive birthday gift. If you're making him as a gift, you could embroider the recipient's initials on the bear's shirt for an extra-personal touch.

Finished Measurements

10" x 11" (including arms, legs, and ears)

Materials

½ yard of solid cotton flannel

Two 5" x 8" pieces of patterned cotton fabric

Small cotton fabric scraps for inside of ears

½ yard of lightweight fusible interfacing

HeatnBond Lite fusible adhesive

Nature-Fil Bamboo Fiber (or Poly-Fil) stuffing

Rickrack or ribbon trim for neckline

5–7 buttons

Coordinating thread

Embroidery floss in various colors and embroidery needle

Basic sewing tools (see page 15)

Pattern Piece A (page 139)

Pattern Piece B (page 139)

Pattern Piece C (page 139)

Prepare the Pieces

Iron the fusible interfacing to the cotton flannel according to manufacturer's directions. Iron HeatnBond to the patterned cotton fabric, which you'll use as the bear's outfit.

Sew and Embellish

NOTE: *All seam allowances are ¼" unless otherwise noted.*

1   Mark and cut two of Pattern Piece A from cotton flannel and set aside. Mark and cut 12 of Pattern Piece B from cotton flannel. (If using a dark fabric, it helps to trace out the pattern on the interfacing side.)

2   Mark and cut two of Pattern Piece C from patterned cotton fabric, then peel off paper backing.

3   Place one Pattern Piece A on an ironing board flannel-side up and top with one Pattern Piece C, adhesive side down. Iron to fuse the layers together. Repeat for the remaining Piece A and Piece C. These will be the front and back pieces of the bear.

4   Pin and sew a length of rickrack or ribbon trim across the raw edge where the flannel and cotton fabrics meet. Do this for both the front and back of the bear.

5   Choose a piece to be the front of the bear and embroider flower shapes, nose, and mouth on the face area, following the placement guide on Pattern Piece A and using a running stitch (see page 19).

6   Hand-sew the button eyes using embroidery floss (I used two buttons stacked for each eye on my bears), then sew three buttons down the front of the bear's shirt. Set the body of the bear aside to work on the limbs and ears.

7   Cut two small fabric scraps using Pattern Piece B, but trim the curved edge ½" smaller than you did with the flannel. Pin to two Pattern Piece Bs and topstitch using coordinating thread. Place six Pattern Piece Bs (including the ones you just added fabric scraps to) flannel side up on table. Top with

the remaining six pieces, placed flannel side down. Pin in place and sew along curved edge, leaving straight side open.

8   Clip notches into the curved corners, then turn right side out and press flat. Topstitch with coordinating thread about ⅛" from the curved edge.

9   Place the front of the bear right side up on the table, then top with arm, leg, and ear pieces, placing them as indicated on Pattern Piece A. Ear pieces should be placed with the fabric scrap side facing the front of the bear.

10 Place the back of the bear right side down on top of the front and pin into place all around the bear's edges. Stitch around all edges of the bear, leaving a 3" opening under the left ear for turning.

11 Clip notches into the curved corners and turn the bear right side out. Press flat to remove any wrinkles, then fill the bear with stuffing. Hand-sew the opening closed with a hidden stitch (see page 19).

Themes and Variations

- **Safety First** If you plan to give this bear to a baby, don't use buttons or trims that could be pulled loose by curious fingers. Use safety eyes and buttons, which stay secure, instead (see Resources, page 141).

- **Sweat It Out** Try making a version of Square Bear using soft felted sweaters—maybe you'll have some leftover from making Silly Snake (page 96)?

- **Family Night** Creating this bear would be a great project to do with kids. If they are too young to sew themselves, let them help choose the fabrics and embellishments that will go into making their bear.

Custom
Vinyl Bib

Babies are tops in their field when it comes to two things: 1) being cute and 2) being messy. Good thing iron-on vinyl was invented! You can use this handy substance to give any fabric you like a slick surface that's super easy to wipe clean. These bibs are so simple to create, you could whip one up for every day of the week—and they're so adorable you may be tempted to wear one yourself! Maybe you'll want to consider making the iron-on coasters featured in Themes and Variations instead.

Finished Measurements

8" x 11"

Materials

Two 9" x 12" pieces of cotton fabric (two different prints)

One 9" x 12" piece of HeatnBond Lite fusible adhesive

One 9" x 12" piece of HeatnBond Iron-On Vinyl (gloss finish)

Rickrack trim

Extra-wide double-fold bias tape

One size 16 ($^7/_{16}$") snap

Coordinating thread

Basic sewing tools (see page 15)

Fine-tip permanent marker

Pattern Piece A (page 140)

Prepare the Pieces

Choose a piece of fabric and iron the HeatnBond to the wrong side according to manufacturer's directions. Once cool, peel off the paper backing and place adhesive side up on the ironing board. Place the second piece of fabric wrong side down against the adhesive and press with iron to fuse.

Sew and Embellish

1 Choose which fabric you want to use for the front of the bib and place it on the ironing board with that side facing up. Apply iron-on vinyl according to manufacturer's directions and allow to cool.

2 Using the template, trace the bib shape onto the vinylized fabric. Cut out using a small rotary cutter, being careful to push through all layers of fabric.

3 Cut a 45–50" length of bias tape and pin into place all around the edges of the bib, starting anywhere on the outer edge of the bib (center bottom works great). Push the ends of the pins so they exit through the bias tape and not the vinyl, otherwise you may leave holes.

4 Topstitch the bias tape all the way around, about ⅛" from the inside edge of the tape. Once you're about 2" away from the starting point, stop stitching (with the needle still in the fabric). Cut the bias tape so it will overlap the starting point by about 1". Fold the end under ½", pin into place, and continue stitching.

5 Cut a 45" length of rickrack and pin into place on the front of the bib, covering the bias tape. Hand-stitch into place with coordinating thread, sewing through the top layer of bias tape only (not through vinyl layers) and overlapping the rickrack's starting point.

6 Mark two spots with permanent marker as indicated on the template. Attach snaps according to manufacturer's instructions.

Themes and Variations

- **Play Picasso** The family fridge isn't the only place to display kiddie artwork—let your baby's older brother or sister draw on plain canvas with fabric markers or crayons, and use this to create the front of the bib.

- **Have a Drink on Me** Create easy coasters using iron-on vinyl. Just fuse a layer of wool felt to a layer of fabric using HeatnBond UltraHold. Then iron vinyl to the top layer (fabric, not felt). Trace and cut squares or circles (using pinking shears or scalloped scissors looks great!). The felt underside will keep your furniture from getting scratched, while the vinyl tops will keep moisture on your drinking glass where it belongs. If desired, you could topstitch the layers together as well for added interest—just be sure to use a non-stick foot (see page 16) so it moves smoothly.

Dainty Doll Quilt

TOO HOT TO HANDLE You can use these same basic directions to make a fun potholder for the kitchen. Just size down the quilt blocks to about 6" x 6" and hand-stitch a loop of scrap fabric to one corner so you can hang it up. Add a layer of Insul-bright heat-resistant padding for safety. Ask for it at your local notions shop.

Odds are, if you have a kid, they have at least one doll—and everyone knows a doll needs a doll quilt! These make fun and unexpected gifts for kids, and making a small-scale quilt is a wonderful way to practice different sewing techniques and experiment with new patterns without having to make a huge human-sized blanket. The technique used to make this particular doll quilt is called Disappearing Nine-Patch, and has a playful and random look that works great with all kinds of fabrics.

Finished Measurements

10" x 10"

Materials

Nine 4" x 4" squares of cotton fabric

One 10" x 10" square of cotton fabric (for the back)

One 10" x 10" piece of Warm & Natural quilt batting

Extra-wide double-fold bias tape (to make your own, see page 18)

Coordinating thread

Basic sewing tools (see page 15)

Sew and Embellish

NOTE: *All seam allowances are ¼" unless otherwise noted.*

1   Place two 4" x 4" squares right side together, then pin and sew along one edge to join. Remove pins and press seam flat. Repeat with a third 4" x 4" square to create a strip of three squares and set aside.

2   Repeat step 1 with the six remaining 4" x 4" squares, creating two additional strips of three squares each.

3   Place two fabric strips right sides together, then pin and sew along one long edge to join. Remove pins and press seam flat. Repeat with the last fabric strip until you have one large nine-patch quilt square. The square should now measure 11" x 11"—trim up the edges with a rotary cutter if necessary.

4   Make two chalk lines through the center of the square: one centered vertically and one centered horizontally. Cut the lines with a rotary cutter. You will be left with four new fabric blocks.

5   Turn the remaining blocks any way you like until you're happy with the arrangement. Place the top two blocks right side together, then pin and sew along the middle edge to join. Remove pins and press flat. Repeat with the bottom two blocks.

6   Place top fabric strip and bottom fabric strip right rides together, then pin and sew along long middle edge to join together. Remove pins and press flat. The assembled quilt square should now measure 10" x 10"—trim up the edges with a rotary cutter if necessary.

7   Place the 10" x 10" backing fabric right side down, then place the quilt batting on top. Top with the assembled quilt square (right side up) and pin all layers together. Sew all layers together, starting by stitching in the ditch (see Tricks of the Trade on page 37) along the center seams. Continue stitching with any pattern you like—I sewed simple diagonal lines from corner to corner.

8   Attach the bias tape according to the directions on page 18, mitering the corners as described.

Spumoni Stripe Quilt

This baby quilt takes its inspiration from an Italian sweet treat called Spumoni, which is made with layers of chocolate, pistachio, and cherry ice creams mixed with whipped cream. The soft colors would be appropriate in almost any nursery and are a welcome change from the typical all-pink or all-blue look. Using fabrics with small-scale patterns ensures that the quilt won't be overwhelming, while the freehand straight stitching adds a subtly off-kilter charm. Rather than attaching a separate bias tape or blanket binding, the backing fabric is folded toward the front to create a self-binding that is both pretty and easy to execute.

Finished Measurements

36" x 48"

Materials

Three 6½" x 36" strips of green fabric

Three 6½" x 36" strips of pink fabric

Two 6½" x 36" strips of brown fabric

One 41" x 53" piece of patterned fabric (for backing)

One 36" x 48" piece of Warm & Natural quilt batting

Quilter's safety pins (see Resources, page 141)

Coordinating thread

Basic sewing tools (see page 15)

Sew and Embellish

NOTE: *All seam allowances are ¼" unless otherwise noted.*

1   Pre-wash your fabrics (see Trick of the Trade, page 108). Place one green strip right side up on the quilt batting, lining up the 36" edges at the top edge. Place a pink strip directly on top of the green strip, right sides together. Pin into place and sew along the bottom edge of the fabric strips, sewing through all layers (including the batting). Remove pins and press flat.

2   Place a brown strip right side down on top of the pink strip you just added. Pin into place and sew along the bottom edge. Remove pins and press flat.

3   Repeat the above steps with remaining strips of fabric, alternating colors like so: green, pink, brown, green, pink. Press seams flat after adding each strip of fabric.

4   Place backing fabric on a large table, right side down. Place quilt top right side up on top of the backing fabric, centering as best you can. Pin all layers together with quilter's safety pins.

5   Starting at one end of the quilt, sew six lines lengthwise on each strip of fabric. It's not important that the lines be perfectly straight—in fact a little crookedness only adds to this quilt's charm. When you reach a seam line between fabric strips, however, try to stitch in the ditch (see Tricks of the Trade on page 37) and keep those lines straight.

6   Remove any remaining pins and press flat. Lay the quilt flat on a table with the striped side facing up.

7   Using a ruler and water-soluble pen, mark a line all around the top of the quilt, ¼" in from the edge. (The edge of the quilt top and batting, not the edge of the backing fabric.)

8   Measure and cut a line 1¼" out from the line you marked in step 7 on the backing fabric, all the way around the quilt.

9 Fold the tips of each corner of the backing fabric down to meet the line you marked in step 7 on the quilt top and press. Open this fold up and trim off each tip at the pressed line. Now turn the corners in toward the front by ¼" and press.

10 Continue turning and pressing all edges of the quilt backing in toward the front by ¼".

11 Starting at one corner, fold one of the quilt's edges in so the pressed edge of the backing lines up with the line you marked in step 7. Press and pin into place.

12 Repeat step 11 along all sides of the quilt, pressing and pinning as you go. As you work you'll see that the folding and pressing creates a diagonal finish that meets up at the corners of your binding.

13 Once all the binding is pressed and pinned, topstitch around all sides of the quilt, about ⅛" from the inside edge of the binding.

14 Hand-stitch the diagonal lines at each corner closed with coordinating thread.

Trick of the Trade

Some quilters don't bother pre-washing their fabrics before they start sewing, but since cotton is known to shrink I always make a habit of it. I don't want to put the work into making a quilt, only to have it come out of the washing machine looking all wonky. Pre-washing also removes any chemicals that might be present (fabric stiffeners and the like) and helps cut down on the chance that your colors might bleed. I recommend pre-washing in cool water with a mild detergent, then drying on low heat. Removing the fabrics from the dryer before they are completely dry will help you press out any wrinkles before you start sewing. Once you've finished sewing your quilt, throw it in the washer and dryer again—but this time, don't press it afterward, since that crinkly look is part of what gives quilts their character.

Chapter 5 · Crafties

Crafties

If you're at the point where using an old shoebox for storage isn't cutting it anymore, try whipping your workspace into shape with one of these crafty organizers. After all, it can be hard to let your creativity run wild when you can't even find your tools—but if you take the time to create a beautiful place to store them, crafting will be that much more pleasurable. Store your crochet hooks in a convenient folding denim holder festooned with a sprinkle of vintage buttons, or corral your knitting needles in a quick-to-make, rickrack-trimmed canister. Bring your needles and thread on the road with you in a colorful, folding needle book, or try your hand at creating a stylish and useful craft apron. Keep your sewing machine dust-free and pretty as a picture with a vintage-inspired cozy, or create a ribbon-strewn pincushion you can wear on your wrist.

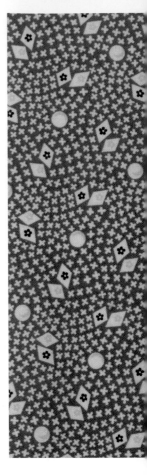

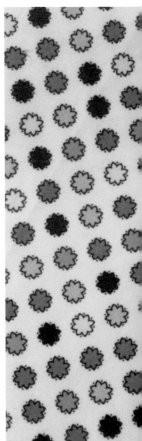

Crochet
Hook
Cozy

These sweet yet sturdy crochet hook cozies are made with denim and lined with bright floral fabric. They hold twelve standard-length crochet hooks, with a flap to keep them extra safe. The pocket is useful for holding small scissors, yarn needles, stitch markers, or any other little notions you may want to keep on hand. Using a colorful vintage button as a closure keeps things stylish and secure. Add a few more buttons for decoration—or try sewing on an embroidered patch or two.

Finished Measurements

Folded: 4½" x 7"

Open: 11½" x 7"

Materials

12" x 11" piece of dark denim exterior fabric

12" x 11" piece of floral cotton lining fabric

8¾" x 4½" piece of floral cotton fabric for flap

3" length of coordinating ribbon

12" x 11" piece of lightweight fusible interfacing

1 button for closure

Buttons for decoration (optional)

Coordinating thread

Basic sewing tools (see page 15)

Prepare the Pieces

Denim exterior fabric: Iron the fusible interfacing to the wrong side of the denim exterior fabric.

Floral lining fabric: Fold the flap piece in half lengthwise, right sides together. Sew one short edge closed. Turn right side out and press flat. Top-stitch along the sewn and folded edges of the flap, ⅛" in from the edges.

CHALK IT UP I like to use a chalk-based liner when marking lines on denim, since it shows up so well and it's easy to clean up using a slightly damp sponge (or you can just let it come out in the wash).

Sew and Embellish

NOTE: *All seam allowances are ¼" unless otherwise noted.*

1   Pin the denim and floral fabric main pieces right sides together, with the denim piece on the bottom and a 12" edge at the top and bottom. Sandwich the flap between the main pieces in the top right corner, with the long raw edge of the flap along the top edge and both raw edges of the flap sticking out from between the main pieces by about ¼". Be sure the flap is on the inside of the bag, so it'll be on the outside when you turn it right side out!

2   Sew all the way around the main pieces and through both layers of the flap, leaving a 3" opening on one side for turning the cozy right side out. Turn the cozy right side out and press flat.

3   Fold the bottom edge up about 3½" and press. Fold the ribbon in half to make a loop and slip the cut ends under the top left corner of your new denim bottom flap. Pin in place and topstitch around the left, top, and right sides of the cozy, ⅛" in from the edges.

4   Using a ruler, mark a vertical line on the denim flap 3½" in from the left (to make one large pocket), then another one 4" in from the right. Topstitch over the lines.

PENCIL IT IN You can also use this organizer to stash colored pencils, makeup brushes, or short double-pointed knitting needles.

5   Mark out five more vertical lines in each pocket below the fabric flap and topstitch over them, creating a total of 12 hook pockets. Feel free to experiment with the sizes of the hook pockets you create. I prefer to make some pockets skinny and some pockets fat so I can fit a variety of hook sizes in them.

6   Fold the hook section in half from the right, then fold the left side over and press to create creases. Hand-sew the button to the front so the ribbon loop hooks over it. Sew other buttons to the front as decoration, if desired.

Knitting
Needle
Canister

It's always a challenge to organize an ever-expanding stash of craft supplies, but before you head to the store to look for help, take a look around your home. This knitting needle canister can be made using a plain old oatmeal container and basic craft supplies you may already have on hand, such as felt and embroidery floss. The end result is a handy new organizer that's much cuter than anything you can buy—and it's a cinch.

Finished Measurements

7" high x 13" circumference

Materials

7" x 14" piece of wool felt

4³⁄₈" x 14" piece of floral cotton fabric

14" length of jumbo rickrack

Two 14" lengths extra-wide double-fold bias tape (to make your own, see page 18)

Coordinating thread

Embroidery floss in contrasting colors and embroidery needle

Basic sewing tools (see page 15)

Empty oatmeal container

Sew and Embellish

NOTE: *All seam allowances are ¼" unless otherwise noted.*

1   Using chalk, mark a horizontal line 3⅝" down from the long top edge of the felt piece. Place the bottom long edge of the floral fabric on the line (right side facing down) and pin in place. Sew ¼" from the bottom edge of the floral fabric, then flip the fabric over and press flat. Topstitch along the top edge of the fabric, ⅛" in from the seam.

2   Place and pin the bias tape onto the bottom and top edges of the cozy, sandwiching the edges of the felt and fabric in the tape to make a binding. Sew in place, stitching ⅛" in from the edges, being sure to catch both the fabric and felt layers in the stitching at the bottom edge.

3   Embroider a line of long running stitches (see page 19) in the felt, ¼" up from the top edge of the fabric panel. Using a second color of floss, embroider another line of running stitches ¼" down from the lower edge of the binding.

4   Hand-stitch rickrack underneath the top edge of the cozy so that the top peaks show from behind the binding.

5   Fold the cozy in half horizontally, right sides together, and pin and sew the raw edges together. Press the seam open, turn the cozy inside out, and slip it over the oatmeal canister.

Themes and Variations

● **Kitchen Confidential** You can easily adapt this method to whip up cozies for all kinds of containers—from soup tins to coffee cans and more. Make the felt base piece as tall as your container and ¾" longer than its circumference.

● **Stash It** Punch a hole in the oatmeal can lid (sanding the edges a bit if they are rough) and use your canister to hold yarn, twine, or ribbon. The hole gives you a place to pull the yarn through while keeping the yarn ball itself from rolling around and getting tangled.

Pockets Aplenty Apron

As far as I'm concerned, you can never have too many pockets—especially when you're in the middle of a big sewing project that keeps you hopping from your machine to the ironing board and all points in between. This apron features a handy fabric loop to keep your scissors at the ready, and there are three large pockets to hold odds and ends like tape measures, pens and pencils, or scraps of fabric.

Finished Measurements

20" x 11"

Materials

One 19" x 19¾" piece of patterned cotton fabric (Piece A)

One 11" x 19¾" piece of denim or canvas fabric (Piece B)

One 8" x 19¾" piece of polka-dot cotton fabric (Piece C)

One 4" x 62" piece of patterned cotton fabric

One 2½" x 7" piece of polka-dot cotton fabric

One 11" x 19¾" piece of HeatnBond UltraHold fusible adhesive (to match Piece B)

One 8" x 19¾" piece of HeatnBond UltraHold fusible adhesive (to match Piece C)

Rickrack trim and embroidery floss (optional)

2 yards of extra-wide double-fold bias tape (to make your own, see page 18)

Coordinating and contrasting thread

Basic sewing tools (see page 15)

Sew and Embellish

1   Place Piece B wrong side up on the ironing board, then place the 11" x 19¾" piece of HeatnBond paper side up on top. Iron together following manufacturer's directions. Peel away the paper backing when cool.

2   Place Piece C wrong side up on the ironing board, then place the 8" x 19¾" piece of HeatnBond paper side up on top. Iron together following manufacturer's directions. Peel away the paper backing when cool.

3   Place Piece A wrong side up on ironing board, then align one of the long edges of Piece B (which is right side up) with one of the long edges of Piece A. Iron to fuse the pieces together.

4   With Piece A still wrong side up on the ironing board, place Piece C right side up over the remaining unfused area of the fabric. Iron to fuse the pieces together.

5   Cut a 19¾" piece of bias tape and pin it to cover the edge where Pieces A and C meet. Topstitch bias tape to edge.

6   Fold the apron at the line between Piece B and C, so the two pieces are facing one another. Press flat and pin together to create one large pocket.

7   Mark two lines on the pocket, 7" in from each side. Stitch along the lines to create three pockets.

8   If desired, pin a piece of rickrack about 1" above the top edge of the pocket and stitch down with contrasting embroidery floss at an angle as shown.

9   Starting at one short edge of the apron, pin bias tape into place to cover side and bottom edges of apron and topstitch to sew layers together, mitering the corners using the directions on page 18.

10 Fold the 2" x 7" piece of polka-dot fabric lengthwise with right sides together and press. Pin and sew the open long edge closed. Use a turning tool (page 13) to turn the fabric tube right side out. Press and topstitch along both long edges.

BUTCH IT UP Skip the rickrack trim and use simple, masculine fabrics to make a guy-friendly version of this apron. It's a great Father's Day gift—just be sure to call it a "toolbelt" instead.

11 Fold the 62"-long strip of fabric in half along the long sides, pressing flat as you go to create one long crease in the middle of the strip. Open the strip back up and fold both long edges in toward the crease and press flat. Fold the strip in half along the long sides and press again, so you end up with a 62"-long strip that is 1" wide. Fold in half (with the short ends meeting) and mark a spot with chalk at the center of your strip.

12 Make a mark with chalk at the center top edge of the apron. Slip the top edge inside the fold of the 62" fabric strip (lining up your chalk marks) to create a belt. Slip the cut ends of your 7" fabric strip (from step 10) under the belt as well, centered over the leftmost or rightmost pocket (your preference). Sew down all open edges of the fabric strip, stitching about ⅓" from the edge.

Nifty Needle Book

This needle book is a simple way to keep your sewing supplies at the ready when you're out and about. Making the pages out of felt means you can stick all kinds of pins and needles into it without mussing it up, and the strip of ribbon gives you a place to tuck embroidery floss and the like. Best of all, these little booklets are so quick and easy to whip up you could make one as a treat for everyone in your craft group.

Finished Measurements

Folded: 4" x 3¾"

Open: 8" x 3¾"

Materials

One 3¾" x 8" piece of patterned canvas (or similar weight) fabric

One 3¾" x 8" piece of wool felt

Two 3" x 6" pieces of wool felt (in two different colors) for the interior pages

One 3¾" x 8" piece of HeatnBond Ultra fusible adhesive

5" length of grosgrain ribbon

One Size 16 snap

Coordinating thread

Basic sewing tools (see page 15)

Scalloped-Edge Rotary Cutter

Fray-Chek fabric sealant

Prepare the Pieces

Apply Fray-Chek to the cut ends of the ribbon and allow to dry.

Iron the HeatnBond to the canvas according to the manufacturer's instructions. Peel the backing paper off and place the canvas sticky-side down on the piece of wool felt. Iron the canvas to the wool until all layers are fused together. Allow to cool, then trim by ¼" all the way around.

Sew and Embellish

1   Topstitch the canvas and felt sandwich assembled piece all the way around, approximately ⅛" from the edge. This is the book cover.

2   Fold the cover in half, canvas side out, and mark a spot on the right-hand edge where you'll add a snap with an air-soluble pen. Add the snap using manufacturer's directions.

3   Cut the short ends of the 3" x 6" pieces of felt with the scalloped-edge rotary cutter. Center the ribbon on one of the pieces of felt and stitch down the ends by hand (or with the sewing machine). Stitch again 1¾" to the right and left of the ends.

4   Lay the cover felt side up. Center the two smaller felt pieces on top of the sandwich and pin into place. Sew down the center.

5   Fill the book with your sewing odds and ends, such as pins stuck through the plain felt pages and thread tucked into the ribbon pages. Fold in half and snap closed.

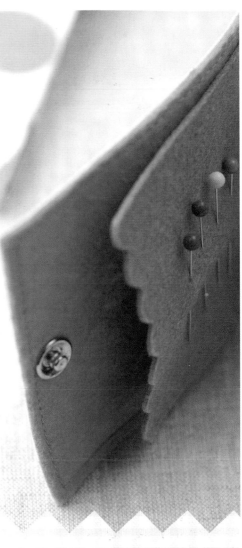

Themes and Variations

- **Personalize It** Before adding the fusible adhesive and ironing the book cover to the felt, add a few embroidered details (such as a monogram or floral shapes) to personalize it. Makes a great gift for the seamstress in your life!

- **What a Gem** These handy little books are also a swell way to organize and transport earrings and small brooches when you're traveling. Since the pages are made from felt, you can push the earring posts and pinbacks right through the fabric.

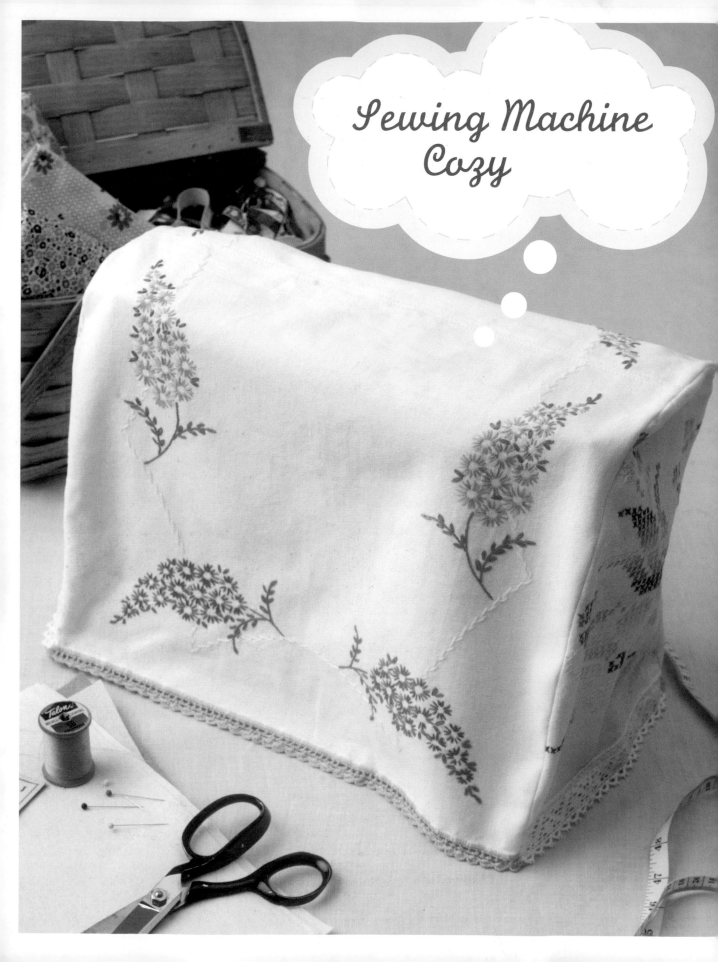

Sewing Machine Cozy

I'm very lucky in that I have a dedicated sewing space at home—I've turned our dining room into my fabric-strewn domain. But just because I'm able to leave my sewing machine sitting out 24–7 doesn't mean I want to look at it all the time. Furthermore, it's really best to keep your machine covered when it's not in use—it keeps the machine free of dust and lint, which means smoother sewing. The good news is this cozy is quick and easy to make. I used vintage table linens to make mine, which were already embroidered and trimmed with pretty lace, but you can use any sort of lightweight fabric you like and embellish it however you want.

Finished Measurements

Approximately 15" x 11½" x 8"

Materials

One 16" x 27" piece of fabric (this will be Piece A)

Two pieces of fabric cut to Pattern Piece B (page 140)

Ribbon trim (optional)

Coordinating thread

Basic sewing tools (see page 15)

Sew and Embellish

NOTE: *All seam allowances are ¼" unless otherwise noted.*

1   Pin one long side of Piece A up and around the curved sides of Piece B. Sew along the edge and press the seams open.

2   Repeat step 1 on the other side of Piece A. Fold the raw edge at the bottom of the cozy in by ¼", press, and sew.

CUSTOM FIT This pattern makes a slightly loose and drapey cozy that will fit a wide variety of machines. Should you want a closer fit for your machine, turn the cozy inside out and sew the seams again with a larger seam allowance for a tighter fit, then snip off any excess fabric.

3   Pin and sew ribbon or trim to the bottom edge, if desired.

Themes and Variations

- **Pocket Pal** To get more storage bang for your buck, you could easily add a pocket or two to your cozy. Just cut a rectangle out of fabric, fold in all the sides by ¼", and press. Stitch along the top edge of your pocket-to-be, then pin it into place on your finished cozy. Sew the sides and bottom of your pocket, then use it to stash pattern pieces or notions.

- **Tea Towel Cozy** If you're really strapped for time, here's one of the quickest ways I know to keep your machine under wraps. 1) Drape a tea towel over your machine. 2) Hand sew two lengths of ribbon to each side. 3) Tie the ribbons in knots. Presto! Instant sewing machine cozy.

Wrist Pincushion

Much to my husband's chagrin, sewing in front of the television is one of my favorite things to do. It's not the sewing itself that bugs him, it's the fact that I tend to leave pins all over the place: stuck in the arms of the couch, embedded in the pillows . . . So I came up with the idea to make a pincushion I could wear on my wrist much like tailors do. The end result was so cute I find myself wanting to wear it even when I'm not sewing—and, best of all, my husband no longer gets jabbed with pins when he sits down.

Materials

Two 3¾" squares of wool felt

Nature-Fil Bamboo Fiber (or Poly-Fil) stuffing

A variety of rickrack and ribbon trims (narrow ones are best, but at least one should be ½" wide)

Coordinating and contrasting thread

Basic sewing tools (see page 15)

Chopstick or similar long, narrow object

Snappy Fabric Bracelet (see page 25)

Sew and Embellish

NOTE: *All seam allowances are ¼" unless otherwise noted.*

1   Sew several strips of ribbon and trim to the top felt square in any arrangement you like. You can sew them on by hand or on the machine, whatever you prefer. Sew rickrack on by stitching diagonally, as shown, if desired.

2   When sewing trims to the square you intend to be the underside of the cushion, start with a ribbon that's at least ½" wide running right down the center. Don't sew this ribbon all the way across. Instead, leave a 1⅝" open space in the middle of the ribbon so you'll have a loop to run a ribbon or Snappy Fabric Bracelet through for wearing. Embellish the rest of the bottom piece of felt.

3   Place the felt squares ribbon-sides together, with the ribbons perpendicular to each other. Pin and sew together all around the edge, leaving a 1½" opening along one side.

4   Turn the cushion right side out and use a chopstick or something similar to push out the corners. Fill with stuffing until the cushion feels firm, then slip-stitch the opening closed with coordinating thread.

5   Slip a Snappy Fabric Bracelet through the open loop on the pincushion's underside to wear it like a bracelet (or just tie it on with a length of ribbon if you prefer).

Themes and Variations

● **Mix It Up** You could also make this pincushion out of a normal cotton fabric, just be sure to iron in some lightweight interfacing first for strength.

● **Follow Your Nose** Skip leaving an opening space to thread a bracelet through and fill the cushion with lavender buds instead of stuffing, and you've got a fragrant little square sachet to scent your dresser drawers.

Templates

4-in-1 Reversible Headband A
enlarge 200%

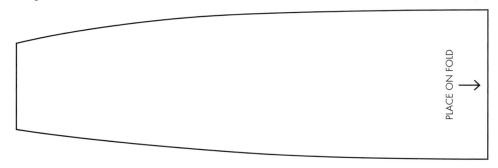

PLACE ON FOLD →

4-in-1 Reversible Headband B
enlarge 200%

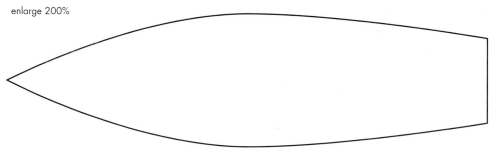

Eyeglasses Cozy A
100% actual size

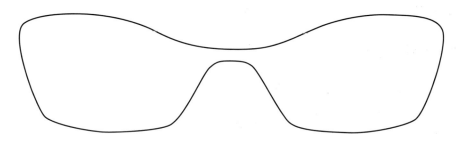

Eyeglasses Cozy B
100% actual size

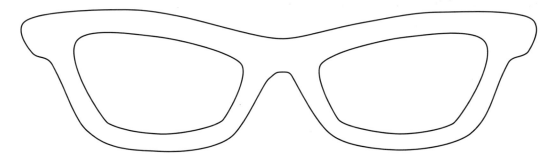

Sweet Treat Appliquéd Tote

ice cream cone enlarge 200%

Sweet Treat Appliquéd Tote

cupcake 100% actual size

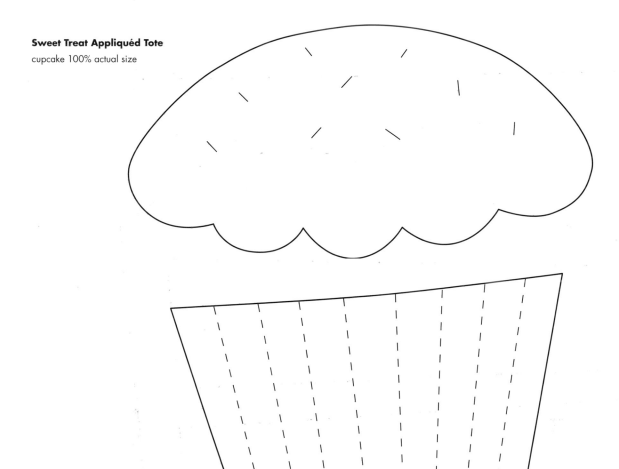

Sweet Treat Appliquéd Tote

layer cake 100% actual size

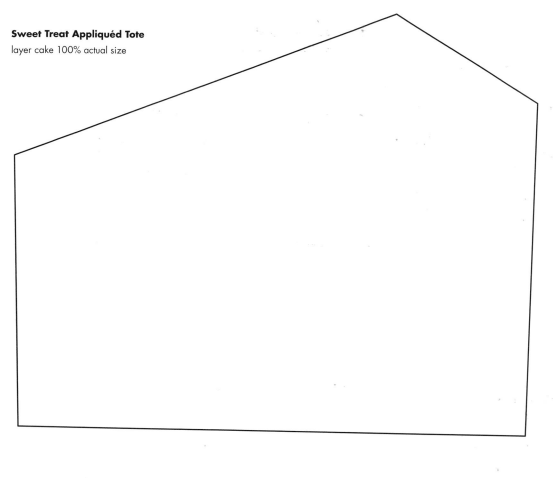

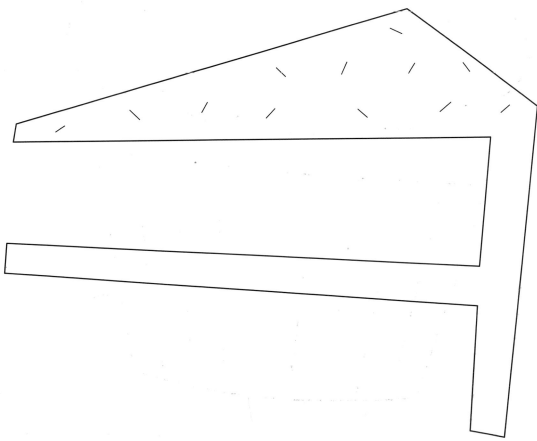

Pillowcase Purse A

enlarge 200%

Merit Badge Wristlet A
enlarge 200%

Merit Badge Wristlet Appliqué
100% actual size

Terrycloth Travel Pouch A
enlarge 200%

Nice View Café Curtain Appliqué
100% actual size

Nice View Café Curtain Appliqué
enlarge 200%

Patchwork Travel Pillow A
enlarge 200%

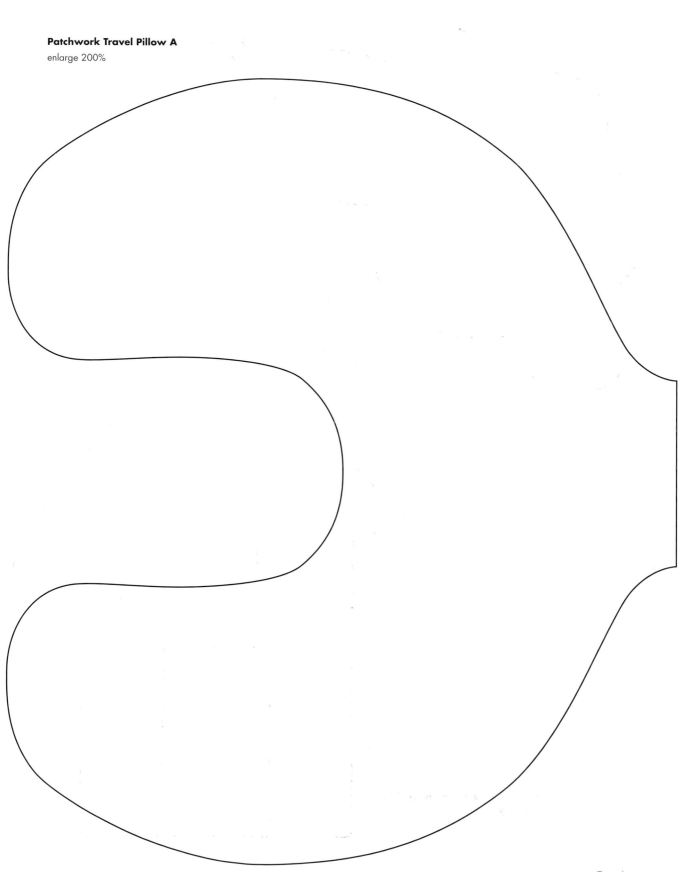

Silly Snake A
head enlarge 200%

Silly Snake B
body enlarge 200%

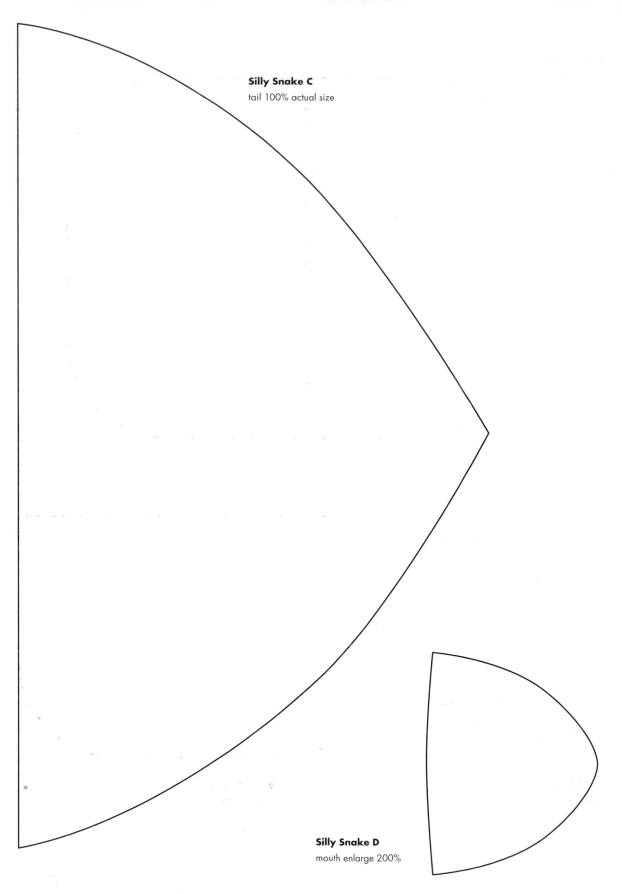

Silly Snake C

tail 100% actual size

Silly Snake D

mouth enlarge 200%

Square Bear A
enlarge 200%

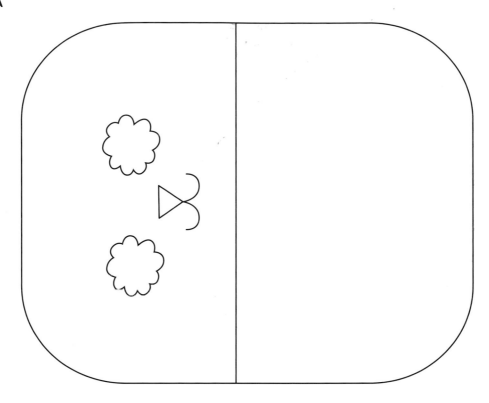

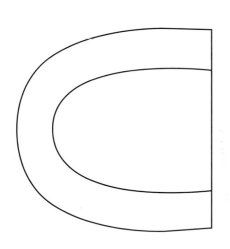

Square Bear B
100% actual size

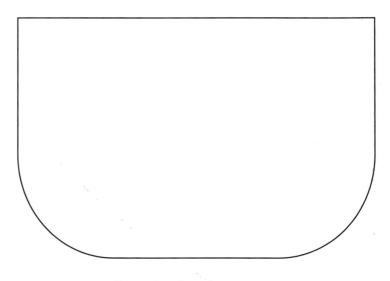

Square Bear C
enlarge 200%

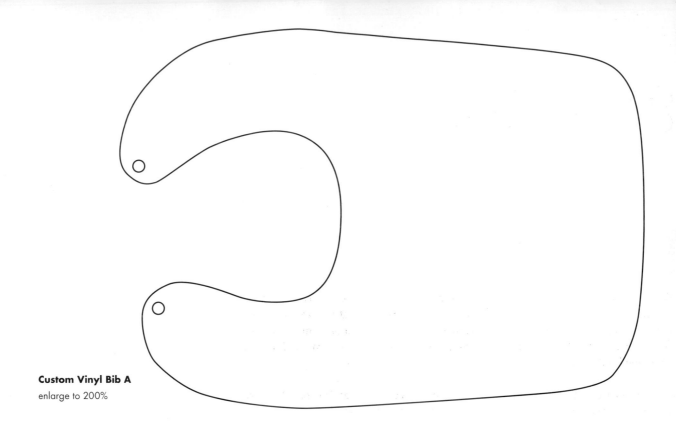

Custom Vinyl Bib A
enlarge to 200%

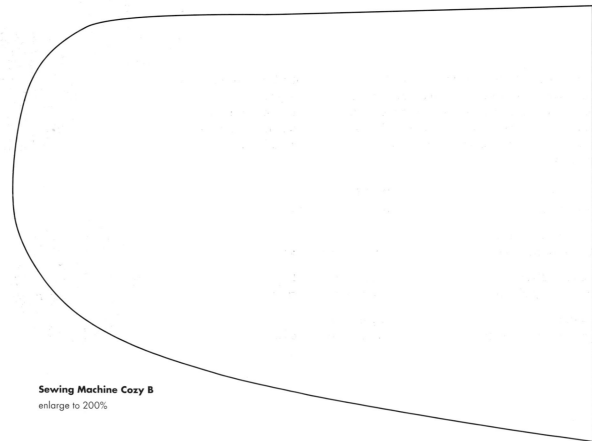

Sewing Machine Cozy B
enlarge to 200%

Resources

VINTAGE FABRICS

Many of the projects in this book were created using vintage fabrics, which I source from all over. To start your own stash of gorgeous vintage textiles, just keep your eyes open. Estate sales and flea markets, thrift shops and grandma's closet—these are all great places to score some one-of-a-kind yardage. Here are some good online sources as well.

Contemporary Cloth
www.contemporarycloth.com

Make Me Fabrics
www.makemefabrics.com

Sharon's Antiques Vintage Fabrics
www.rickrack.com

The Tin Thimble
www.thetinthimble.etsy.com

FABRICS

Not everyone has the luxury of living in a town with a great fabric shop (though if you do have one nearby, I hope you'll support them and shop locally). The Internet is an endless resource for great fabric shops; here's a list of the ones I frequent most. Remember to check the Notions and Tools sections of these sites too, as they're often full of helpful items like yo-yo templates and bias tape makers.

e-Quilter
www.equilter.com

The Fat Quarter Shop
www.fatquartershop.com

Hancock's of Paducah
www.hancocks-paducah.com

J. Caroline
www.jcarolinecreative.com

Purl Patchwork
www.purlsoho.com

Reprodepot Fabrics
www.reprodepot.com

Sew, Mama, Sew!
www.sewmamasew.com

Superbuzzy
www.superbuzzy.com

CHARMS/TRIMS

Atomic Veggie
www.atomicveggie.com

The Buzzard Brand
www.thebuzzardbrand.com

Les Bon Ribbon
www.lesbonribbon.com

Naughty Secretary Club's "Crafty Curios"
www.naughtysecretaryclub.etsy.com

Tinsel Trading Co.
www.tinseltrading.com

Vintage Necessities
www.vintagenecessities.etsy.com

NOTIONS & TOOLS

Foamerica
www. foamerica.com

Kit Kraft
www.kitkraft.biz

Nancy's Notions
www.nancysnotions.com

The Snap Source
www.thesnapsource.com

PATTERNS

Betsy Ross
www.betsyrosspatterns.com

Sublime Stitching
wwwv.sublimestitching.com

INSPIRATION & TUTORIALS

Cathy of California
www.cathyofcalifornia.typepad.com

Craft Magazine
http://blog.craftzine.com

Crafty Chica
www.craftychica.com

CraftyPod
www.craftypod.com

Knick-Knacks & Ric-Rac
www.madewithlovebyhannah.com/WordPress

ScrumDillyDilly
www.scrumdillydilly.blogspot.com

MEASUREMENT EQUIVALENCIES

Inches	Centimeters
¼ in	0.6 cm
½ in	1.25 cm
1 in	2.5 cm
1 ft	30.5 cm
1 yd	91.4 cm

Index

Acknowledgments

I'm not sure there are words adequate enough to express my gratitude towards the folks who made this book happen—but I'll try. My deepest thanks to Sharyn Rosart, Erin Slonaker, Sarah Scheffel, Lana Le, Ryan Willis, and Lynne Yeamans for their endless reserves of enthusiasm, patience, and wisdom. Thanks also to the team at Bill Milne Photography for making me feel so at home and for taking such beautiful photographs of my work, and to the team at St. Martin's for being as excited about this book as I am.

Last but not least, thanks to all my friends and peers in the craft world and beyond for your encouragement and support. You're all lifetime members of Team Sew Darn Cute!